Critical Guides to French Texts

Critical Guides to French Texts

EDITED BY ROGER LITTLE, WOLFGANG VAN EMDEN
DAVID WILLIAMS

MAURIAC

Le Nœud de vipères

Kathleen M. McKilligan

Lecturer in French
University of Keele

Grant & Cutler Ltd
1993

ISBN 0 7293 0358 6

I.S.B.N. 84-599-3328-8

DEPÓSITO LEGAL: V. 2.950-1993

Printed in Spain by
Artes Gráficas Soler, S.A., Valencia
for
GRANT & CUTLER LTD
55-57 GREAT MARLBOROUGH STREET, LONDON W1V 2AY

Contents

To my Mother

Prefatory Note

All references to *Le Nœud de vipères* are to the commonly used student text edited by John T. Stoker and Robert Silhol, London, Harrap, 1959.

Italicised numbers in parentheses, followed by page references, refer to the other numbered items in the Select Bibliography.

I should like to take this opportunity of expressing my gratitude to Dr Graham Pick for invaluable encouragement and assistance during the preparation of this study.

Biographical Note

François Mauriac was born in Bordeaux in 1885, the youngest of five children. His father died when he was twenty months old, leaving his mother a widow at the age of twenty-eight. She took the children to live on the third floor of a house in Bordeaux belonging to her mother, where two female cousins also lived. The bachelor brother of her late husband was the only male influence on the children's upbringing. The family lived in several different houses in Bordeaux during François's childhood, while he attended a Catholic kindergarten and then a school run by the Marianist religious order. This profoundly Catholic education, together with his mother's strong spiritual influence, gave the young boy a deep religious faith which he would never lose, despite various crises in later life.

School holidays were spent in the country, never far from Bordeaux by modern standards, in various country houses belonging to relatives. Mauriac thus developed a great love and knowledge of the countryside of the Bordeaux region and of the area south of Bordeaux known as Les Landes, which he was to make world-famous as the setting for several of his novels.

He completed his school education by a short spell at the Lycée de Bordeaux before entering Bordeaux University where he took an arts degree. After graduating, he moved to Paris in 1907 with the plan of studying to become a specialist librarian and archivist at the École des Chartes, but although he did study there, he soon became involved in Parisian literary circles and gave up his librarianship plans in favour of becoming a writer. He published his first book, a volume of poetry called *Les Mains jointes*, in 1909, and was thrilled when it received an enthusiastic review from the well known right-wing author Maurice Barrès. He was also involved with several literary and religious periodicals.

In 1913 he married Jeanne Lafont, daughter of a well-to-do banker. Their first child, Claude, who was himself to become a distinguished novelist and writer, was born the following year, and two daughters and another son followed over the next ten years. The year of his marriage also saw the publication of his first novel, *L'Enfant chargé de chaînes*, and another appeared the following year, when the First World War brought a break in Mauriac's literary career. Although exempt from military service on medical grounds, Mauriac joined the ambulance service, and served as an orderly with the Red Cross first in northern France and later in Salonika, where he contracted malaria and was invalided home in 1917. The following years saw Mauriac's career as a novelist get well under way, with three more novels appearing by 1921, and fame finally assured once he won the Grand Prix du Roman in 1925 for *Le Désert de l'amour*. In 1927 he published *Thérèse Desqueyroux*, the novel which rivals *Le Nœud de vipères* as his best. *Le Nœud de vipères* itself was written in 1931, and was a great success when it appeared the following year.

Are there any particular reasons why Mauriac should have written *Le Nœud de vipères* in 1931? In the mid-1920s, in his early forties, Mauriac had undergone a major spiritual crisis, which was resolved through his encounter, towards the end of 1928, with the abbé Altermann, a Catholic priest who was instrumental in the conversion of many French intellectuals. While it would not be accurate to say that Mauriac experienced a 'conversion' at this time, he was beyond doubt deeply immersed in the conflicts between the demands of the earthly and the spiritual, as is evident from his non-fiction writings of the period (for instance, *Dieu et Mammon*, 1929).

In June 1929 Mauriac's beloved mother died, and a few months later he began a short novel, *Ce qui était perdu*, completed the following spring. Suffice it to say here that this novel portrays characters who are torn apart by violent personal conflicts which undoubtedly owe something to the turmoil recently experienced by Mauriac. It also explores the intervention of divine grace in a much less subtle way than in *Le Nœud de vipères*, the next novel Mauriac embarked upon. While *Ce qui était perdu*, unlike *Le Nœud de vipères*, is not a book of major public appeal, it marks Mauriac's emergence from an extremely troubled personal period which culminated in the masterpiece that is *Le Nœud de vipères*. As Jacques Monférier puts it, '*Le Nœud de vipères*, composé en 1931, marque la fin de cette période, qu'il n'est pas excessif de qualifier de tragique' (20, p.7).

Shortly after the publication of *Le Nœud de vipères* in 1932, Mauriac was found to be suffering from throat cancer. He underwent a successful operation, but the realisation that his illness might have proved fatal spurred him to write, later the same year, *Le Mystère Frontenac*. This is a semi-autobiographical portrait of a family very different from that pictured in *Le Nœud de vipères*, an Mauriac himself said in 1951 of his reasons for writing it: 'Si j'avais dû mourir, je n'aurais pas voulu que *Le Nœud de vipères* fût le dernier de mes livres' (see 2, t.II, p.1237).

Mauriac was elected to the Académie Française in 1933, but his period of regular novel production was past, although *La Pharisienne* in 1940 and *Un Adolescent d'autrefois* in 1969 were still to be added to his list of best-sellers.

In all, Mauriac wrote twenty-two novels and four plays, as well as various short stories, essays, biographies and several volumes of memoirs. He was also a prolific contributor to newspapers and reviews, and was always outspoken when he thought injustice was being done, even when it meant embracing a minority or unpopular view. He died in Paris in 1970, at the age of 84, mourned as one of the greatest literary figures of twentieth-century France.

1. Louis: Narrator and Protagonist

i) Narrator and Narrative

The first chapter of a Mauriac novel is usually of vital importance to the whole, and *Le Nœud de vipères* is no exception. Without any preliminaries, the opening line of *Le Nœud de vipères* takes the reader straight to the heart of the novel: 'Tu seras étonnée de découvrir cette lettre dans mon coffre sur un paquet de titres' (p.37). The attentive reader will spot the feminine ending of *étonnée*, and the familiar *tu* form, which, together with the reference to *les enfants* in the following sentence, make it seem likely that the letter is addressed to the narrator's wife.

That it is no sentimental letter of last farewell is made abundantly clear by the first few sentences, in which the narrator visualises his family seizing the deeds to his property as soon as he has breathed his last. His own attitude is equally unloving, for he delights in telling his wife how, at one time, he had plotted secretly to ensure that his family should not inherit his fortune. 'Vous avez eu la chance que je survive à ma haine', he tells her (p.37), or rather his family, since the *tu* of the start here gives way to the plural *vous*, the narrator's dreams of vengeance being aimed at the entire family. When his hatred had been at its peak, he continues, he even used to lie awake at nights dreaming of how he could himself enjoy the family's dumbfounded consternation when they discovered he had disposed of his fortune. If he got his timing right, he had thought, perhaps he could permit his family to open his empty strong-box just before he died, in time for him to gloat over their dismay: 'Il me semblait alors que la plus atroce agonie ne me gâterait pas ce plaisir', he recalls (p.38).

The very idea that someone should attempt to visualise the circumstances of his own death in such terms is profoundly shocking. As an opening to the novel, it is likely to make the reader continue out of sheer curiosity, which is precisely what Mauriac intends.

Note the subtle change in past tense usage in the conclusion of this introductory section, as the narrator asks the question which he will proceed to answer in Part I of the novel: 'Oui, *j'ai été* un homme capable de tels calculs. Comment y *fus-je amené*, moi qui n'*étais* pas un monstre?' (p.38). The descriptive imperfect *étais* designates what the narrator thinks was his original state, while the perfect tense *j'ai été* is used for the state in which he had been during a certain time, now ended. Most importantly, the past historic of the passive *fus amené* suggests that he believes certain outside forces, at a particular moment, had operated to change his original personality.

All three of these time-states are examined as the novel progresses, as well as the time during which Louis is actually writing, for much will happen as the narrative takes shape. The narrator moves frequently from one time state to another, and the reader may find it helpful to analyse the sequences as he goes along. Helena Shillony, who has done just this, concludes that Part I of the novel, which is dominated by the 'passé éloigné', serves as 'une exposition qui prépare et explique l'action dramatique' of the second part, where the present and recent past tenses predominate (see *23*, pp.82–85).

Let us not be deceived by the use of the word 'lettre' in the novel's first sentence. While the letter form provides a useful starting-point for the narrator's story, there is little of the epistolary genre in *Le Nœud de vipères*, apart from the occasional use of the second person singular in personal remarks to his wife, Isa, and the 'genuine' letters from Hubert and Janine which conclude the book. Moreover, the whole of Part II, which is not much shorter than Part I, is written after the narrator has dropped any pretence of writing for his wife's benefit: 'ces pages ne s'adressent plus à personne' (p.131).

In fact, Louis has already recognised the true nature of his narrative as early as the start of Chapter III: 'Ce n'est plus une lettre, mais un journal interrompu, repris...' (pp.52–53). A little later, in Chapter V, Louis admits that the nature of what he is writing has changed: 'Sortirai-je jamais de cette histoire? Je l'ai commencée pour toi (...). Au fond, c'est pour moi-même que j'écris' (p.77). The cathartic function of pouring out one's problems, whether to an imaginary ear (or eye, in Isa's case), is of course undeniable. Through self-exploration Louis will come to self-understanding, an aspect of the narrative we shall look at later, in Chapter Four.

Critics have devoted a considerable amount of time to discussing whether *Le Nœud de vipères* should be considered a letter, a confession, an autobiography or memoirs, and not surprisingly most of them conclude that the novel is a mixture of some or all of these genres. If we wish to categorise the style of the narrative, why not follow the example of Mauriac himself, who some twenty years after writing the book described it as 'une lettre-réquisitoire... qui tourne au journal intime' (see 2, t.II, p.884)?

We must remember, too, that Louis is a lawyer by profession. It is scarcely surprising that much of his narrative reads like an eloquent self-defence, aimed at making us take his side against the family. Even Hubert, not usually very perceptive, understands this: 'Cet avocat n'a voulu perdre son procès, ni devant lui-même, ni devant nous', is Hubert's cynical comment on his father's manuscript (p.210). Mauriac puts legal terminology into Louis's mouth too: 'Vieil avocat, je mets en ordre mon dossier, je classe les pièces de ma vie, de ce procès perdu' (p.77).

It is important not to confuse Mauriac with the narrator. When we examine the writings of Louis, what we are really examining are the efforts of Mauriac to allow the reader to see into the mind of his protagonist. However much we feel we are penetrating the innermost thoughts of Louis, ultimately it is Mauriac who directs the narrative.

Take, for example, the blank spaces which separate blocks of narrative within the chapters. These spaces in the text, slightly larger than those between paragraphs, are deliberate but unobtrusive structuring devices. Sometimes a blank may indicate a break in time, as for instance in Chapter 1 when Louis starts writing again after stopping because of poor light: 'Il a fallu que je m'interrompe...on n'apportait pas la lampe; on ne venait pas fermer les volets' (p.40).

Similarly, after the introductory block of Chapter III, the blank marks a whole night's pause, as well as a change of heart: 'Je relis ces lignes écrites hier soir dans une sorte de délire. Comment ai-je pu céder à cette fureur?' (p.52). In other places, the blank merely marks the start of a new presentation. The second block of Chapter III, for example, concludes 'Souviens-toi de notre première rencontre', followed by a blank before Louis starts on his happy recollections of Isa in Luchon (p.53).

It should be noted that no divisions existed in Mauriac's original manuscript, neither chapter divisions nor the division into two parts, nor, for the most part, even paragraph divisions. These were all added at the last minute, as part of preparing the text for its readers. The best way of appreciating the value of such divisions is to visualise how the book would look without them, and how much more difficult it would be to follow the story's development. The chapter divisions and the blanks are no mere convention, like paragraphing, but rather markers which facilitate the transition from one episode to another.

This structuring of the *récit* is part of Mauriac's skilful manoeuvring to show the reader exactly what he needs to know, no more and no less. Mauriac is an economical novelist: he does not digress from his central theme or give us insignificant details. The novel is carefully constructed so that the maximum amount of information in conveyed as concisely as possible, yet so skilfully is this done that we feel it is Louis who is gradually disclosing his innermost thoughts to us. The almost imperceptible slide from letter to confession and self-analysis is peculiarly apt for Mauriac's purpose, since it gradually reveals more and more of Louis's true nature and his slow progress to self-understanding.

ii) *Louis as Child, Adolescent and Student*

A closer examination of the narrative shows us how Mauriac, although invisible behind his narrator, organises Louis's self-disclosure with great care. Louis starts writing on the afternoon of his 67th birthday, which happens to be the Thursday of Holy Week, prompted to do so by some strange impulse, possibly because his family always ignores his birthday — a reference which is of course designed to make us feel sorry for him (p.39). He continues next day, noting that the usual angelus bell has not rung, which is Mauriac's way of underlining that it is Easter Friday (p.62). This substantial section constitutes the first three chapters, and allows Louis to fill in the details of his family, upbringing, and engagement to Isa. Thus while the novel has no introduction as such, Mauriac sets out all the background information necessary to understand Louis's reaction to Isa, and his subsequent disillusionment.

An only child, Louis had been brought up with immense, even overpowering, devotion by his widowed mother, who came of a thrifty peasant family. She and her husband, a local government official, had had her family's unproductive grazing lands planted with pines, which, by the time Louis came of age, were valuable mature trees, producing pit props. This is, incidentally, historically correct for much of the region known as the Landes, south of Bordeaux: an infertile and marshy region, it was largely planted with pine trees during the nineteenth century to drain the land whilst also producing a commodity in demand in the coal-mining industry. Louis's parents had also invested successfully in the other major agricultural product of the Bordeaux region, by scrimping and saving to buy the vineyards of Calèse, later so dear to both Louis and his mother.

Despite a comfortable childhood, Louis believes he and his mother are poor, and never loses his innate thriftiness. Even once he is a wealthy lawyer, for instance, he eats in the cheapest restaurants in Paris, despite the dreadful food, because of his 'terreur de trop dépenser' (p.158). It is too late to change when, in his late teens, his mother triumphantly reveals the truth about their fortune. This revelation coincides with a shattering blow: Louis had dreamed of becoming a teacher, but illness brought on by overwork had ruined his hopes just two months before the competitive entrance examination to the École Normale. In retrospect, Louis realises he had missed out on the fun of childhood: 'Quand je lis les souvenirs d'enfance des autres, quand je vois ce paradis vers lequel ils se tournent tous, je me demande avec angoisse: "Et moi? ..." Hélas, je ne vois rien que cette fureur acharnée, que cette lutte pour la première place, que ma haineuse rivalité avec un nommé Hénoch et un nommé Rodrigue' (p.46).

Yet Mauriac shows us no reason to blame anyone but Louis for this. His mother had tried in vain to get him out into the fresh air instead of poring over his books. At school, he had shied away from any boys who tried to befriend him: 'Mon instinct était de repousser toute sympathie...J'avais horreur des "sentiments"' (p.46). It is not difficult to see here the formation of the crusty old man before us.

His mother's loving concern for him had irritated him constantly during his year of convalescence on the Atlantic coast at Arcachon, where the air was thought at that time to be particularly helpful to patients with chest complaints. 'Oui, j'étais atroce', Louis recalls: 'dans la petite salle à manger du chalet, sous la suspension qui éclairait nos repas, je ne répondais que par monosyllabes à ses timides questions; ou bien je m'emportais brutalement au moindre prétexte et même sans motif '(p.49). As always, his mother had borne his behaviour with patience, making excuses for him, and showering him with money. Her indulgent attitude, of course, simply stores up trouble for the future by making Louis even more self-centred.

Only in later years does Louis appreciate his mother's love, even seeing a kind of ironic justice in the fact that later he is starved of the love which had so irritated him as a youth. As a young man, however, he had blamed his mother for his unhappiness, just as later he blames Isa: 'A tort ou à raison, j'en voulais à ma mère de ce que j'étais. Il me semblait que j'expiais le malheur d'avoir été, depuis l'enfance, exagérément couvé, épié, servi.' And just as later he will not keep his feelings hidden from Isa, neither does he show any mercy towards his mother: 'Je fus, en ce temps-là, avec elle, d'une dureté atroce. Je lui reprochais l'excès de son amour' (p.48).

Where relationships outside the home were concerned, Louis had been his own worst enemy. His inferiority complex led him to act in such a way that his worst fears were confirmed: 'Je me hâtais de déplaire exprès par crainte de déplaire naturellement' (p.48). He had always been ill at ease in groups, incapable of joining in jokes: 'Je glaçais les gens, par mon seul aspect...: j'appartenais à la race de ceux dont la présence fait tout rater' (p.48). With the opposite sex he had been equally unsuccessful: 'Je prenais avec les femmes, par timidité et par orgueil, ce ton supérieur et doctoral qu'elles exècrent...Plus je sentais que je leur déplaisais et plus j'accentuais tout ce qui, en moi, leur faisait horreur' (p.48).

Louis's feelings of social inadequacy lead indirectly to his hatred of the Catholic church. At Bordeaux University (where Mauriac had himself been a student), Louis cannot help being jealous of his fellow-students' background and education: 'C'était [*sic*, but 'C'étaient' in 2, II, p.396] presque tous des fils de famille, élevés chez les jésuites et à qui, lycéen et petit-fils d'un berger, je ne pardonnais pas l'affreux sentiment d'envie que leurs manières m'inspiraient, bien qu'ils m'apparussent comme des esprits inférieurs' (p.50). Although previously Louis had paid no attention to religion, the jealousy inspired by his fellow students now leads him deliberately to condemn the religion which their families embrace.

Catholicism, for the young Louis, is one of the marks of a social status which he cannot attain, until he meets Isa in Luchon, that is, when he accepts that going to mass with her is a necessary part of his new status. While an undergraduate, however, Louis had to make do with the companionship of students who, like himself, were 'fils de petits fonctionnaires, anciens boursiers, garçons intelligents et ambitieux mais pleins de fiel' (p.51). Although with his newly discovered fortune he did not lack followers, and founded a successful discussion group where he learned to excel in public speaking, Louis made no real friends, for, as he admits himself, 'au fond je ne les méprisais pas moins que les bourgeois. Je leur en voulais de manifester naïvement les misérables mobiles qui étaient aussi les miens, et dont ils m'obligeaient à prendre conscience' (p.51). Since deep down Louis despises himself and the jealousy he feels, he is over-sensitive to similar feelings in others.

iii) Louis and Isa

Mauriac deliberately dwells on Louis's unhappy, insecure youth so that the reader can appreciate the sudden joy that Louis feels when he believes the daughter of the socially superior Fondaudège family has fallen in love with him: 'Tout d'un coup, j'avais la sensation de ne plus déplaire, je ne déplaisais plus, je n'étais pas odieux' (p.55). His mother's shrewd assessment of the Fondaudèges is in vain: ' "Tu ne vois pas que ces gens cherchent à t'attirer?" répétait-elle, sans se douter qu'elle risquait ainsi de détruire mon immense joie d'avoir plu enfin à une jeune fille' (p.56).

It is worth noting here that the actual name 'Louis' appears rarely in the novel, only on Isa's lips when she is worried or concerned about him (pp.71, 149, 150). Significantly, too, Mauriac gives Louis no surname, unlike Isa, whose name of Fondaudège symbolises much that Louis feels he lacks. Although in later years Mauriac said he wished he had given Louis a surname (see *4*, p.94), this comparative anonymity of the narrator was probably no accident at the time. The novelist is concerned with the narrator's mind and the narrator as an individual, not with his external appearance or what others think of him, whereas Isa is used more as a symbol of family and class attributes than as an individual.

Louis does not fall in love with Isa. To realise this is vital for understanding why the marriage goes sour just because Isa mentions her previous fiancé. Louis is totally egocentric, and the main value of his relationship with Isa is that it changes his own self-image. His recollections concentrate on 'cette merveilleuse découverte que je faisais: être capable d'intéresser, de plaire, d'émouvoir' (p.56). Of Isa's feelings we hear virtually nothing, nor does Louis tell us how

wonderful he thought she was: 'L'amour que j'éprouvais se con-
fondait avec celui que j'inspirais, que je croyais inspirer. Mes
propres sentiments n'avaient rien de réel. Ce qui comptait, c'était
ma foi en l'amour que tu avais pour moi' (p.56).

Since their relationship depends on the inner glow created by
Isa's apparent love of Louis, the reader is forewarned of disaster as
soon as Louis suspects her motives. Although at the time Louis is
delighted when he becomes engaged to Isa almost by accident, in
retrospect he sees her 'misunderstanding' as part of her plot to
secure a replacement for her lost fiancé. Incidentally, there would
seem to be a minor discrepancy in dating on Mauriac's part here,
since the engagement happens in August 1883, while the honey-
moon and the subsequent discovery about Rodolphe are placed in
1885 (see pp.53, 54, 66, 71). Louis's *récit*, however, suggests that
the wedding took place quickly and quietly, with the Fondaudèges
using the death of a distant relative as an excuse for not publicising
their daughter's marriage into a family of which they were
ashamed.

As newly-weds, Louis and Isa are extremely happy. Louis's
mother barely recognises him: 'Nos fous rires l'étonnaient: ce jeune
mari heureux, c'était pourtant son fils, si longtemps fermé, si dur'
(p.67). That their happiness should be wrecked by Isa's explanation
about Rodolphe is entirely Louis's fault. So convinced is he of his
own worthlessness that he instantly puts the worst possible interpretation on Isa's enthusiasm for him: 'Tu l'avais pris, ce malheureux,
parce qu'il se trouvait là, cette année où ta mère, en proie au retour
d'âge, s'était persuadée que tu n'étais pas "mariable", — parce que
tu ne voulais ni ne pouvais demeurer fille six mois de plus, parce
qu'il avait assez d'argent pour que ce fût une suffisante excuse aux
yeux du monde...' (p.71).

Louis's newly created self-respect, his vision of himself as
lovable and desirable, is shattered. No matter what Isa says about
Rodolphe, Louis interprets all her remarks as unfavourable to
himself. When Isa protests that Rodolphe would not have been a
faithful husband as he was too handsome and attractive to other
women, Louis reflects bitterly that he is the opposite: 'Cela signifiait

que moi, je serais ta joie grâce à mon visage ingrat, à cet abord revêche qui éloignait les cœurs' (p.71).

To the reader Isa's naïve explanations are not unconvincing: she had seen Louis as the answer to her prayers, and had ignored the snobbish protests of her brother-in-law, Baron Philipot. 'Mais je tenais à toi, mon chéri, il en a été pour ses frais', she tells Louis with some satisfaction, assuring him that she has no regrets (p.70).

Louis is not so much jealous of Rodolphe as suffering from a shattered ego from which he will never recover, although there is doubtless some self-delusion in his assurances that 'il n'y avait pas en moi trace de jalousie' (p.71). When he gets up, he looks at himself in the mirror, 'comme si j'eusse été un autre, ou plutôt comme si j'étais redevenu moi-même: l'homme qu'on n'avait pas aimé' (p.72).

Shortly after the 'Rodolphe' episode — 'avant les vendanges', we are told, since the cycle of the vines is the major marker in Louis's existence — Isa suffers a miscarriage. This marks the start of a difficult period for Isa, but one which Louis takes advantage of: 'ces années de gestations, d'accidents, d'accouchements qui me fournirent de plus de prétextes qu'il n'était nécessaire pour m'éloigner de toi' (p.76). Instead of offering love and support, Louis uses Isa's pregnancies and miscarriages as an excuse for launching into 'une vie de secrets désordres'. In thinking that his extramarital affairs were unknown to Isa, however, Louis is deluding himself, since it turns out years later that she had simply preferred to turn a blind eye to them.

To the reader, it is scarcely surprising, in such circumstances, that Isa should have turned to her children for comfort. Yet Louis accuses her of having abandoned him: 'Dès la naissance d'Hubert, tu trahis ta vraie nature: tu étais mère, tu n'étais que mère. Ton attention se détourna de moi' (p.76). The arrival of the children, like the mention of Rodolphe, attacks Louis's self-esteem: Louis sees love as exclusive, like his mother's single-minded love for him, and cannot conceive that Isa should still love him while extending her love to the children.

The comparison between his mother and his wife is one which Louis makes himself. Although he has had a very satisfactory career, he blames Isa for the fact that it has not been even better: 'Si j'avais eu, à ce moment, une femme qui m'eût aimé, jusqu'où ne serais-je pas monté?' (p.84). What he needed, he thinks, was someone to encourage him, to mark up his successes, 'comme autrefois, à la distribution des prix, chargé de livres, je cherchais des yeux maman dans la foule et au son d'une musique militaire, elle déposait des lauriers d'or sur ma tête frais tondue' (p.85).

Louis is of course too selfish to realise that he has offered Isa no support whatsoever in her maternal role. More crucially, he does not realise that what he complains of in Isa is precisely what he praises his mother for, namely selfless devotion to her children. His mother had received equally little in return from him: indeed, when she declines in old age, Louis only notices this in relation to himself, when he complains that she is more interested in her pet dog than in him. Louis expects constant attention and availability from those who love him, but he has nothing to offer in return.

In a first person narrative, we have to rely on the narrator for all our information about the other characters. From Louis's point of view, and therefore that prevailing on the reader, Isa is entirely to blame. It is important to remember, however, that what we see may be biased, and that Louis's reports and interpretation of events, or even of remarks, may not always be accurate. Even when he reports direct speech, he may be selecting the remarks which best fit in with the view he personally has of the individual speaking.

This is particularly important when we are considering the character of Isa. All our information about her comes from what Louis tells us, with one very important exception, namely the fragments of burnt correspondence he finds after her death, fragments which show she believed him to have had an affair with her sister Marinette. There is manuscript evidence, incidentally, that Mauriac intended at one point that Luc should indeed be the offspring of such an affair, but this was omitted in the final version (see *8*, p.88, n.23).

Although Louis had considered having an affair with Marinette, it had been purely in a spirit of 'getting even' with Isa, much as at Arcachon he had deliberately pursued a girl whom he did not even like, simply because he knew it distressed his mother. When he pieces together the burnt fragments, however, Louis is triumphant to an unseemly degree on discovering his wife had been jealous of Marinette and had feared that Luc was his son. At long last, Louis is convinced that Isa must have cared for him: 'Elle avait souffert par moi; j'avais eu ce pouvoir de la torturer...je jouissais de n'avoir pas été indifférent à une femme, d'avoir soulevé en elle ces remous' (p.191). This is essential to our understanding of Louis: what mattered most to him was his effect on others, and it was what he had imagined to be Isa's indifference and lack of love towards him that had poisoned his marriage.

What of Louis's other relationships? His greed, insecurity, and fear of being used had stopped him from embarking on the type of love affairs that a man of his professional standing could have had without difficulty. No longer believing in love, he had found satisfaction with prostitutes, with whom he could feel he was merely striking a financial bargain: 'J'aime que tout soit tarifé; oserais-je avouer cette honte? Ce qui me plaisait dans la débauche, c'était peut-être qu'elle fût à prix fixe' (p.89).

In retrospect he is disgusted by it all. 'C'est ainsi que j'ai compris "l'amour"', he reflects bitterly: 'donnant, donnant... Quel dégoût!' This is important, for one of the functions of Louis's narrative is to underline to himself, as well as to the reader, just what a tragic waste his life has been.

It is greed not only for money, but for the kind of single-minded devotion he had received from his mother, which wrecks Louis's chances of any real loving relationship. On the one occasion when he had had what might genuinely be described as a love affair, he had been excessively demanding, until the woman — a grateful client who had fallen in love with him — could stand it no longer: 'C'était ma chose. Mon goût de posséder, d'user, d'abuser s'étend aux humains. Il m'aurait fallu des esclaves' (p.90). Louis is, however, not entirely honest in his self-accusation. Here he makes it seem as if his mistress had left merely because of his possessiveness, but later he reveals another reason: 'mon amie était partie enceinte, pour se cacher à Paris...' (p.131).

Louis tells us what he wants to tell us, or rather what Mauriac wishes him to tell us, at any given point in the book. To hold back until Part II the news that Louis has an illegitimate son suits Mauriac, since it opens up new possibilities for Louis's dreams — soon to be dashed — and provides yet another example of Louis's stinginess, in the way he has treated the boy and his mother.

The nature of Louis's narrative allows Mauriac to insert material at the point where it can best contribute to our understanding of the narrator's character. Thus it is with the 'affaire Villenave', the episode which not only makes Louis famous overnight but also convinces him finally that his wife does not love him, since she shows no interest in his resounding success. Some years after his marriage, in 1893, Louis had acted for the defence of Madame de Villenave, a hitherto devoted wife, who claimed to have shot her husband, in an extraordinary case which had fired the public imagination. Louis, while convinced of Madame de Villenave's innocence, did not understand what had happened, until at the trial he suddenly realised that she was confessing to her son's crime, in order to save the family name.

Incidentally, this is one of the episodes Mauriac uses to anchor his tale in the real world, since Louis tells us, without boasting, that his inspired insight into the son's jealousy of his father had led directly to Freud developing his theories on adolescent psychology (that 'le professeur F.' is indeed meant to indicate Freud is confirmed by the original manuscript — see 2, t.II, p.1192).

Madame de Villenave's enormous self-sacrifice — made not for the sake of her son but for love of her husband, who had begged her to take the blame _ made an unforgettable impression on Louis, who compared her marriage to his own: 'J'aurais pu être un homme aimé comme l'était Villenave... Qu'avait-il de plus que moi?' (p.84).

As usual, Louis's self-interrogation does not go very far. Initially, as we have seen, his marriage had been happy, and it was Louis himself who had put a brutal end to that happiness. Typically, he persuades himself in retrospect that Isa's mention of Rodolphe had not been entirely to blame, that it had been her subsequent treatment of him which had decided the course of their life: 'Il ne me semble pas que je t'ai haïe dès la première année qui suivit la nuit désastreuse. Ma haine est née, peu à peu, à mesure que je me rendais mieux compte de ton indifférence à mon égard, et que rien n'existait à tes yeux hors ces petits êtres vagissants, hurleurs et avides' (p.82).

Later Louis discovers that he had been wrong in assuming that Isa had put her children first. During their last ever talk together Isa weeps at the mere idea: 'Mes enfants! quand je pense qu'à partir du moment où nous avons fait chambre à part, je me suis privée, pendant des années, d'en avoir aucun avec moi, la nuit, même quand ils étaient malades, parce que j'attendais, j'espérais toujours ta venue' (p.149). In this final talk between Louis and Isa, just before Louis goes to Paris to make his fortune over to his illegitimate son, Mauriac deliberately summarises much of what Louis has already told us, but with Isa's reactions too, so that for the first time we glimpse her view of their marriage.

Louis's eyes are also opened to the latter for the first time: 'Un doute me vint, à cette minute-là. Est-il possible, pendant près d'un demi-siècle, de n'observer qu'un seul côté de la créature qui partage notre vie?' This is of course precisely what Louis has done, and we hold our breath as Louis stands on the brink of reconciliation. With unwitting irony he ponders the matter: 'Se pourrait-il que nous fassions, par habitude, le tri de ses paroles et de ses gestes, ne retenant que ce qui nourrit nos griefs et entretient nos rancunes?' (p.149). Alas, the reader realises that this is exactly what Louis is fated to do: he pushes aside his last niggling doubt.

Louis thus ignores Isa's last advances, and when he takes up his pen again, in Paris, it is as if he had decided to ban her from his thoughts: 'Celle pour qui je me livrais, ici, jusqu'au fond, ne doit plus exister pour moi' (p.131). The ambiguity of the remark is possibly designed to reflect the confusion in Louis's own mind. Indeed, it is all too easy to read this passage, the start of Part II of the novel, as if it were written after Isa's death. It seems Louis is now so intent on disinheriting his family that he has to try to stop thinking of Isa, for when he does, the memory of their last walk together makes his resolve falter as he senses the futility of his battle: 'Et voici que dans cet après-midi pesant, les deux adversaires sentaient le lien que crée, en dépit d'une si longue lutte, la complicité de la vieillesse. En paraissant nous haïr, nous étions arrivés au même point' (p.147).

Louis is undoubtedly tempted by the notion of reconciliation: indeed, another reason why he might wish to purge Isa from his thoughts at this point is that he may be reacting against the preceding pages of his *cahier*, where, in the middle of the night, he had toyed with the idea of attempting a reconciliation by begging her to read his manuscript. As on other occasions, however, he rejects what he had written, the next time he takes up his pen: 'N'étais-je pas au bord de la folie?' (p.131).

iv) Louis as a Father

Louis's description of his children as 'petits êtres vagissants, hurleurs et avides', mentioned above, is in itself a giveaway: he could scarcely be described as an enthusiastic father! On his own admission, he paid no attention to his offspring 'tant que les enfants furent des larves' — another significant choice of vocabulary. When they were older, he began to disagree with Isa over their upbringing but this was, he freely admits, the result not of any parental instinct but merely of the jealousy he felt at their devotion to their mother: 'Oui, j'ai cherché à te les prendre pour te punir' (p.76).

This is, incidentally, one instance of Louis becoming more lucid through self-examination, since he can now accept that his motives were not as high-minded as he had pretended at the time: 'Je me donnais de hautes raisons, je mettais en avant l'exigence du devoir. Je ne voulais pas qu'une femme bigote faussât l'esprit de mes enfants. Telles étaient les raisons dont je me payais. Mais il s'agissait bien de cela!' (pp.76–77).

Significantly, we see little of Louis's children, only occasional anecdotes about their childhood or about family gatherings during the actual writing of Louis's manuscript. The only one whom we see directly, through his own words rather than Louis's, is Hubert, in the long, self-satisfied letter he writes to his sister Geneviève at the end of the book.

As Louis had expected, Hubert is incapable of understanding his late father's emotions as expressed in the manuscript. 'Ces pages fielleuses...ne nous révèlent rien, hélas! que nous ne sachions de longue date', he tells Geneviève (p.208). Self-righteous as ever, Hubert remains convinced that, without his own painstaking efforts, his father would never have handed over his fortune. Indeed, so great is Hubert's capacity for finding what suits him in Louis's manuscript that we may wonder if we have read the same *cahier* as he has. For Hubert, his father's claim to have become totally detached from the things of this world is laughable, merely Louis's way of pretending that he had not lost to the family after all — his way to 'transformer sa défaite en victoire morale'. As we see Hubert congratulating himself, we in our turn cannot help but smile as he smugly declares: 'Non, là je ne m'y laisse pas prendre' (p.210).

Most extraordinarily of all, however, to the reader who has seen the extreme lucidity of the mental agonies Louis has suffered, Hubert believes that the manuscript shows beyond doubt that his father had not been in full possession of his senses. Accordingly, he wants Geneviève to destroy the *cahier*. He even — and here Mauriac the author is playing one of his rare jokes on us — imagines with horror the possibility of this incriminating document being published one day: 'Il y a là des indications psychologiques, et même des impressions de nature, qui dénotent, chez cet orateur, un don réel d'écrivain. Raison de plus pour le déchirer. Imagines-tu un de nos enfants publiant ça plus tard? Ce serait du propre!' (pp.211–12).

Neither does Mauriac miss the chance of poking fun at Hubert's good opinion of himself. Hubert thinks Geneviève may, like her daughter, be impressed by what he dismisses as Louis's 'faux mysticisme': 'N'y a-t-il pas trace, me demanderas-tu, de vrai christianisme dans son cas? Non: un homme, aussi averti que je le suis de ces questions, sait ce qu'en vaut l'aune' (p.212). To the reader, who has just witnessed Hubert's total lack of insight, his pompous description of himself as 'un homme, aussi averti que je le suis de ces questions' cannot help but be comic.

To underline the humour, Mauriac allows Hubert to hit the nail on the head, for once, with his assertion — from which, however, he draws a false conclusion — that 'l'étalage de ses [Louis's] aspirations religieuses est une critique directe, ou détournée, des principes que notre mère nous a inculqués dès l'enfance' (p.212). Unlike his more perspicacious niece, whom he refers to pityingly as 'la pauvre petite', Hubert does not realise that 'nos principes demeuraient séparés de notre vie' (p.216), and that Louis had spied a very real gap between theory and practice.

We must acknowledge, however, that Hubert's bitter memories of his father are mostly justified. When Hubert recollects that 'Le mépris que j'inspirais à mon père a empoisonné mon adolescence. J'ai longtemps douté de moi...' (p.208), we get a glimpse of the sort of father Louis had been.

Louis is equally contemptuous of his illegitimate son Robert, in whom he discerns characteristics which he dislikes in himself. The people he admires are his opposites, lively and fearless young men like Luc, and even to some extent Phili, who both in their very different ways refuse to conform to the family stereotype. Likewise, it is only when Janine for the first time refuses to listen to her parents that Louis's attitude towards her softens. Previously, he has always disliked her, considering her insincere, a person who 'emprunte des opinions sur tout et ne comprend rien à rien' (p.78).

Yet Louis is perhaps not entirely to blame for his inadequate relationships with his children. He recollects that whenever Geneviève, as a little girl, had come on to his knee, her mother had called her away (p.81), which suggests Isa deliberately interfered in their relationship. If this were true, however, why had the same not happened with Marie, the only one of his children that Louis had a good relationship with? It is tempting to conclude that, once more, Louis is trying to blame Isa for a failure of his own.

While the comments Louis makes about Geneviève as a grown woman are certainly not complimentary — he describes her as a 'grosse femme de quarante ans', who likes speaking in 'phrases toutes faites' (pp.81, 82) — he shows no hatred towards her, and little of the scorn he undoubtedly has for Hubert. Yet he has no sympathy for her when she tremblingly begs him to help her son-in-law financially in order to save Janine's marriage, nor when she refers scornfully to her own husband's lack of business success. Although Louis claims 'c'est affreux de faire peur à ses enfants' (p.79), it is difficult to believe he is sincere, since even as he makes this remark he is engaged in thwarting his family yet again.

Louis's relationships with his children are inextricably linked to his love of money. He is convinced that it is only by remaining 'le maître de la fortune' that he is secure as head of the family. Those who have read *La Terre* by Emile Zola, written less than fifty years before *Le Nœud de vipères*, will remember the story of the old peasant murdered by his family once he had handed over his money to them, and Mauriac makes Louis express a similar fear: 'Les histoires de paysans qui laissent mourir leurs vieux de faim après qu'ils les ont dépouillés, que de fois en ai-je surpris l'équivalent, avec un peu plus de formes et de manières, dans les familles bourgeoises!' (p.62). Louis's obsession with money is so great that it symbolises his entire existence; he is convinced, for most of the book, that 'un vieillard n'existe que par ce qu'il possède' (p.62). It is only when he frees himself from this conviction that he becomes capable of reacting like a normal human being.

In conclusion, most of Louis's poor relationships with others can be blamed only on himself, although the way in which he tells his story seeks to make us believe that it is others, especially Isa, who are at fault. Since we rarely have the opportunity to hear their side of the story, we as readers are likely to feel sympathetic towards Louis — despite his unpleasant characteristics — which is what his creator Mauriac intends.

2. The Natural and Physical Setting

When the French think of François Mauriac, they think of south-west France. Mauriac was born and brought up here, and set most of the action of his novels here, in the region to the south-east of Bordeaux. He is a regional novelist in another sense too, in that he portrays characters typical of that region, whose working life or family fortune depends on activities prominent in the area, such as vine-growing, the wine trade or the timber industry. In addition, Mauriac's protagonists tend, like himself, to be deeply rooted in their native soil, and to identify very strongly with the landscape around them. As we shall see, this is particularly true of Louis in *Le Nœud de vipères*, for whom the surrounding landscape seems at times to reflect precisely his own emotions.

i) The Setting of the Novel

(a) Calèse

One of the reasons Mauriac evokes the atmosphere of the house at Calèse and its surroundings so convincingly is that it is a real place for him, for Calèse is based very closely on his own home, Malagar. The Malagar estate is situated not amidst the pine forests of Les Landes, where Mauriac had spent his holidays as a child, and which he uses as a setting for several of his novels, such as *Thérèse Desqueyroux*, but some fifty miles further north, on the northern side of the River Garonne. This is the vine-growing region known to wine-lovers as L'Entre-Deux-Mers, where between the waters of the 'seas' of the Rivers Dordogne and Garonne the gently undulating countryside is covered with vineyards as far as the eye can see.

Mauriac's paternal grandfather had settled here, first of all in the town of Langon, by the railway from Bordeaux along the north bank of the Garonne. Later he had acquired the house and estate at Malagar some miles to the north-east, near the small pilgrimage village of Vézelay. Although Malagar passed in due course to Mauriac's mother, she and her children had mostly spent their holidays at her other country house, on the edge of the village of Saint-Symphorien in Les Landes, but in 1927, a few years before Mauriac wrote *Le Nœud de vipères*, she gave the Saint-Symphorien estate to her son Pierre, and the Malagar estate to his younger brother François.

From that time on, Malagar became Mauriac's favourite home, and the place where he did much of his writing. The house still stands today, surrounded by trees, on the brow of a steep hillside of vines that stretches downward towards Langon and the Garonne valley. From it, the long railway viaduct at Langon is clearly visible, the same viaduct Louis refers to in the novel as proof that he can hear perfectly adequately: 'Tu m'as dit, l'autre jour, que je devenais dur d'oreille. Mais non: j'entends le grondement du train sur le viaduc. Non, non, je ne suis pas sourd' (p.52).

At the rear of the house is the famous terrace, where Mauriac's own family gathered on warm summer evenings, and which plays such an important part in *Le Nœud de vipères*. From the parapet, there is indeed a fine view over the valley to Langon by the river, and in the far distance to the south can be seen the dark outline of the forests of the Landes. Louis is describing a sight very familiar to Mauriac when he tells how he and his sister-in-law, alone of all the family, would brave the midday heat to stroll along the terrace to admire the view: 'Nous nous accoudions au parapet de la terrasse (...). La plaine, à nos pieds, se livrait au soleil dans un silence aussi profond que lorsqu'elle s'endort dans le clair de lune. Les landes formaient à l'horizon un immense arc noir où le ciel métallique pesait' (p.107).

Louis seems happiest outdoors, and is greatly frustrated when confined to his room, as he so often is when telling us his story. Yet he has the biggest room, with the best view, facing out over the terrace, and is aware that it is coveted by Geneviève (p.38). Louis remembers sleeping in this room as a child, and expects to die there.

It was there that the fatal mention of Rodolphe had happened: 'C'était dans cette chambre où j'écris aujourd'hui. Le papier des murs a été changé; mais les meubles d'acajou sont restés aux mêmes places; il y avait le verre d'eau en opaline sur la table et ce service à thé gagné à une loterie' (p.42).

Of the house itself we see little apart from Louis's room. It is significant that it is only after Isa's death that we see her room, almost as if it is the first time Louis has entered it. Indeed, he looks around him almost as if it were unknown to him. The grate of the big stone fireplace is hidden by a large painted screen which Louis had damaged with his penknife one day as a little boy, a rare reminder of his childhood, but one which underlines the continuity of human existence. It is unusual for Louis to tell us such details, but Mauriac is leading up to the vital discovery Louis makes behind the screen, namely Isa's burnt letters, and it is therefore important that Louis should notice the screen and try to put it in its correct position.

There is in fact little description as such in the novel. As Bernard Chochon puts it, what interests Mauriac is 'non pas le paysage en tant que tel mais sa relation aux personnages' (*8*, p.55). Mauriac evokes the house at Calèse through its impact on Louis, not by straightforward description.

(b) Other Places

With the exception of Luchon, places other than Calèse seem to have made little impression on Louis. Luchon, or Bagnères de Luchon, to give it its full name, is of course significant because he meets Isa there. Mauriac is clearly writing from personal experience in his remarks about this spa town in the Pyrenees, which he had visited on a family holiday as a boy. The Hotel Sacarron, where Louis and Isa meet, really exists, in the Allées d'Etigny where it is situated in the novel. The references to the Casino, to the bandstand on the square in front of Les Thermes, the actual spa building, to trips up the valley of the Lys river, or to Superbagnères in the mountains above Bagnères de Luchon itself, are all accurate details which bring Louis's experiences there to life for us.

As in several of Mauriac's novels, the city of Bordeaux figures in the book merely as the background for the protagonist's childhood, as it had been to Mauriac's own. Louis's father, who had died before the boy was old enough to remember him, had worked at the Préfecture in Bordeaux, and Louis was brought up in a third floor flat in the rue Sainte-Catherine, which is the name of a real street in the centre of Bordeaux. After his illness in his late teens, he and his mother move to a much more impressive 'hôtel', or town house, 'sur les boulevards', but we see little of Louis's existence here.

The same is true of the scenery of Arcachon, mentioned merely as 'cette forêt sèche, pleine de genêts et d'arbousiers' (p.47). Indeed, the scenes of Louis's childhood seem to have made no lasting impact on him whatsoever: all he remembers is how unhappy he generally was. He tells us, for instance, that 'de lugubres mois s'écoulèrent dans ce chalet d'Arcachon' (p.46), since it was the collapse of his academic ambitions, not the sudden change of scenery, that had the greatest effect on him. We might note in passing that Mauriac, in referring to the seaside villa where Louis spent his convalescence as 'ce chalet d'Arcachon', is using a detail from his own youth: as a child, Mauriac used to spend the school holidays in a house his mother owned in the Landes, but which was built in the chalet-style of the seaside villas of Arcachon, quite different from that of other local houses.

It is significant, I think, that Louis — who in old age is hypersensitive to nature and the world around him — fails to react to, or at least to recollect, his surroundings before his meeting with Isa. It is as if he has to awaken as a person before he can relate to the external world. In Luchon, not only does he first begin to feel valued as an individual through his relationship with Isa, but for the first time he relaxes sufficiently to notice the beauties of nature, and the sounds and smells of the world around him. This sensitivity to the natural world — which he does not seem to have had at Arcachon — will remain with him, although it is always strongest at times of happiness.

Towns, on the other hand, are places of work and business, and make little impression on Louis's memory. In Paris, Louis feels greatly frustrated in his cramped hotel room: 'Entre le lit et l'armoire, à peine ai-je la place de m'asseoir pour écrire' (p.132). Ironically, of course, it is because of his own greed that he has chosen to stay in such a cheap hotel, 'sous prétexte', as he readily admits, that his son Robert and his mother live in this part of Paris, Montparnasse. He hates the noise and bustle of Montparnasse, however, and thinks longingly of home when kept awake by the music and dancing on the eve of Bastille Day: 'Ce soir, treize juillet, un orchestre joue en plein vent; au bout de la rue Bréa, des couples tournent. O paisible Calèse!' (p.134).

It should be noted that Mauriac's references to Paris are no less accurate than the situation of 'Calèse' (Malagar). The Rue Bréa really exists, joining the Boulevard Raspail close to its junction with the Boulevard du Montparnasse, and only a few hundred yards away from the busy Montparnasse mainline railway station. Scarcely surprising, therefore, that Louis should find it so noisy. The other Parisian streets mentioned are also genuine, and accurately situated, such as the Rue des Petits-Champs, where Robert works in a draper's firm, and which is in a busy commercial district off the Avenue de l'Opéra. The stroke of luck by which Louis happens upon the rendezvous of his son and son-in-law in a café — out of all the cafés in Paris! — is made less of an improbable coincidence by the fact that the café in question is the Deux Magots, a well known establishment which might easily be chosen by provincials hastily thinking of some convenient spot to meet. If the choice of the nearby church of Saint-Germain-des-Prés for their secret meeting with Robert seems rather far-fetched, it becomes less so when we remember that, after all, the plotters have good reason to believe that wherever Louis may be in Paris, he is certainly not likely to be in a church!

Another stuffy hotel room Louis remembers is in Luchon, many years before: 'Comme après tant d'années elle demeure présente à ma mémoire, cette chambre étouffante de l'hôtel, cette fenêtre ouverte sur les allées d'Etigny!' (p.59). There, however,

Louis had enjoyed the sounds of the outdoors, of carriages with their drivers singing as they went, which he heard 'à travers les jalousies fermées', and it is his elderly mother, suffering from a migraine, who silently swallows her disappointment about her son's proposed marriage, much as in his turn Louis will regret his son Robert's lack of initiative.

Listening to sounds of the outdoors from indoors, as in the above example, is a frequent occurrence in the novel. At Calèse, since much of the time Louis is alone in his room, one of the aspects of the outside world that impinges on him most is what he hears. His memory of Sundays when the children are small, for example, starts with the noise outside which used to wake him, and which evokes for us the family life from which Louis feels so isolated: 'Les chevaux s'ébrouaient. On appelait la cuisinière qui était en retard. Un des enfants avait oublié son paroissien. Une voix aiguë criait: "C'est quel dimanche après la Pentecôte?"' (p.94). At this stage, of course, Louis isolates himself by choice from the activities outside, whereas by the time of writing it is his poor health which prevents him from participating.

Apart from Louis's dislike of the city, the main reason we see Calèse so much in his recollections is that it has always been the main scene of his confrontations with Isa and his interactions with his children. 'A la ville je n'étais jamais là' (p.91), Louis tells us, always having his work as an excuse, but as the school holidays in summer coincided with the closure of the law courts, all the family were together at Calèse in August and September.

Interestingly, Mauriac makes Louis ask himself the very question the reader may well be asking: 'Pourquoi ai-je toujours passé mes vacances avec vous au lieu de voyager?' (p.95). Louis admits the reason is largely his innate sense of economy: why waste money in hotels, when for nothing he can join the rest of the family at Calèse? I would suggest, however, that there is a deeper reason, which Louis only realises later. Despite his constant arguments with Isa, he needs her, and to some extent justifies his existence by his bickering with her. Once she is dead, Louis feels the whole *raison d'être* has gone out of his life, as it has from his *cahier* of explanation, destined for her. There is also the natural attraction of Calèse where Louis finds a kind of happiness amongst the vines despite his family rows.

ii) Nature and Emotion

Indeed, the view from Calèse always inspires a sense of peace in Louis, or at least inspires him to think of wider issues than his own petty problems. He is quite surprised, after he has made over his fortune to his children, to find that the pleasure of looking at the land and things growing around him has not changed. Whereas he had always assumed it was the feeling of possessing things which made them important to him, he now realises that it must result from a more fundamental human instinct: 'Tout m'intéresse comme au jour où Calèse mappartenait (…). Le bruit de la pluie, la nuit, sur la vendange pourrissante, ne me donne pas moins de tristesse que lorsque j'étais le maître de cette récolte menacée. Ce que j'ai pris pour un signe d'attachement à la propriété, n'est que l'instinc charnel du paysan, fils de paysans, né de ceux qui depuis des siècles interrogent l'horizon avec angoisse' (p.187).

Louis's personal, inner, evolution as he writes the book follows the cycle of nature, from his awakening to the idea of personal change in the spring, through its fruition in the height of the summer, to fulfilment with the grape harvest and the advent of winter, bringing apparent death. Incidentally, it is interesting to note that Mauriac wrote the novel at approximately the same rhythm and over the same period as the dates of Louis's *cahier* beginning and ending slightly earlier in the year, but still over a seven or eight month period between early spring and autumn.

The link with the natural cycle is stressed in Chapter XVIII when Louis is revelling in his new-found peace after dividing his money up amongst his family. He reflects that grapes can never recover from the wrong weather conditions, but his new optimism leads him to believe that man is different in this respect: 'Nous nous réveillons en plein automne et les grappes, où un peu de pluie demeure prise et brille, ne retrouveront plus ce dont les a frustrées l'août pluvieux. Mais pour nous, peut-être n'est-il jamais trop tard. J'ai besoin de me répéter qu'il n'est jamais trop tard' (p.188).

This remark, it would seem, is made after Louis has discovered Isa's burnt letters which change his opinion of her (although in the novel, it immediately precedes and introduces this episode). The following section, after Louis has rushed downstairs, quite forgetting his bad heart, and out into the vineyards, is the greatest set piece of the book. It is late afternoon on a sunny September day, and the grape harvest is in progress. The evening haze is just settling over the countryside, and Louis leans weakly against a stake, 'fâce aux pâles étendues de brume où des villages avec leurs églises, des routes et tous leurs peupliers avaient sombré. La lumière du couchant se frayait un difficile chemin jusqu'à ce monde enseveli' (p.191).

It is with equal difficulty that the light seems to be dawning on Louis, for he has just realised, although he has not yet fully taken it in, that he has never understood Isa, or even guessed at her feelings of unhappiness and insecurity. Louis, like the rays of the dying sun, needed to penetrate the covering mists that hid the real person from sight, yet he had never thought of this before: 'Jamais l'aspect des autres ne s'offrit à moi comme ce qu'il faut crever, comme ce qu'il faut traverser pour les atteindre' (p.191). If only he had made this discovery earlier, how different his life might have been: 'C'était à trente ans, à quarante ans, que j'eusse dû faire cette découverte. Mais aujourd'hui, je suis un vieillard au cœur trop lent, et je regarde le dernier automne de ma vie endormir la vigne, l'engourdir de fumées et de rayons. Ceux que je devais aimer sont morts; morts ceux qui auraient pu m'aimer' (pp.191-92).

The chiasmus of this last sentence, with *aimer* and *morts* being repeated in reverse order in the second part, stresses the two concepts which have become all that matters to Louis now: love and death. He is only too conscious that like the sun his time is almost over, but unlike nature he cannot start afresh. Yet it is not his own death which preoccupies him, but the fact that others — principally Isa, of course — are dead, and hence he cannot demonstrate his new feelings.

It might be argued, of course, that the comparison between the sinking sun and the dying man is too facile, too obvious a way for Mauriac to underline his character's reflections. Yet the daily cycle of the sun has fascinated man since earliest times, and we have seen how close Louis is to nature. Looking out over the landscape around Calèse always makes Louis think about the major perspectives of life, and moreover, in this particular instance, Mauriac ensures there is no hint of sentimentality by having Louis immediately question his thoughts himself: 'Etait-ce précisément ces pensées que je remâchais, appuyé contre ce piquet de vigne, à l'extrémité d'une rège, face aux prairies resplendissantes d'Yquem, où le soleil déclinant s'était posé?' (p.192). The use of a specialised term like *rège* for a row of vines also keeps us firmly on the ground.

Mauriac rounds off the whole episode by extending the metaphor of death into one of sleep, as Louis returns to the house, 'pénétré jusqu'au cœur par la paix qui remplissait la terre'. In the evening mist, the very hills have taken on a human shape: 'Au loin, les côtes perdues ressemblaient à des épaules courbées: elles attendaient le brouillard et la nuit pour s'allonger peut-être, pour s'étendre, pour s'endormir d'un sommeil humain' (p.192). Here, Mauriac is using nature as an extension of his protagonist: Louis too is tired, very tired, both physically and in terms of weariness with the world. Sleep and death are as one for him, and he accepts the inevitable just as surely as night will follow day. Like the landscape, he will sink gratefully into the shadows, with peace in his heart, just as the hillsides are doing: 'le monde entier n'était qu'acceptation'.

Despite the agony of his discovery that it is too late to put things right with Isa, Louis is now assured that all he can do is accept the natural cycle of life, love, and death. Now he must look only forward, and make what amends he can in the time remaining, although his clumsy efforts are not very successful, as the following episode with the servants demonstrates.

Another important scene where nature is used to highlight Louis's emotions is the night of Isa's 'confession'. The heat was so great that they had, unusually, left the shutters open, so that they could hear the leaves of a lime tree brushing against the house, sounding as if 'quelqu'un respirait au fond de la chambre' (p.67). This 'quelqu'un', for Louis, is the ill-defined figure of Rodolphe, who he feels is constantly coming between him and his wife, even as they lie together: 'Il surgissait, ce Rodolphe inconnu, que j'éveillais dans ton cœur, dès que mes bras se refermaient sur toi' (pp.67–68). The moonlight coming in through the open window shows up Louis's hands, 'ma grande main noueuse de paysan, aux ongles courts' (p.68), making him all too conscious of his lack of elegance compared with the picture he creates in his mind's eye of the Cambridge-educated Rodolphe.

The remainder of the night is a nightmare for the shattered Louis, yet outside life continues regardless. A blackbird sings, swallows chatter up on the roof, cocks crow, church bells ring, and in the distance a train rumbles over the viaduct. The stress laid on the normality of the new day underlines Louis's agony: for him it means the end of his brief spell of happiness and the start of the misery of the rest of his life. In addition, the stark contrast between the beautiful morning and Louis's black dejection brings home to the reader that Louis's misery is of his own making: if he trusted his wife, he would not be thus carried away by imagining the worst.

One of the functions of natural phenomena in *Le Nœud de vipères* is to emphasise the durability of nature compared with the transitoriness and fragility of man. Life around Louis continues as before, and as it will continue for years to come: 'Je regardais naître ce jour nouveau, ce jour de ma nouvelle vie. Les hirondelles criaient dans les tuiles. Un homme traversait la cour, traînant ses sabots. Tout ce que j'entends encore après quarante-cinq années, je l'entendais: les coqs, les cloches, un train de marchandises sur le viaduc; et tout ce que je respirais, je le respire encore: ce parfum que j'aime, cette odeur de cendre du vent lorsqu'il y avait eu, du côté de la mer, des landes incendiées' (p.72). At the time of writing, Louis is just as sensitive to the sounds and smells of the countryside as he had been when a young man, yet he is very conscious of growing old, of his decreasing physical ability, while nature remains as ever, the seasons pursuing their course even as Louis sinks towards the end of his life.

Like Isa's confession, some of the most important landmarks
of Louis's life take place at night, or at least in the evening. One
such is the major family discussion about Louis and his money
which he overhears, and which causes his abrupt departure for
Paris. Although it is after one o'clock in the morning, it is still
warm, and the family are sitting outside in front of the house, 'du
côté du perron', namely the opposite side from the terrace where
they usually sit. Only the toilet and corridor windows face this way,
so that no one expects Louis to overhear. On this occasion, it is the
dark outline of the elms that Louis notices, not the lime trees which
come close up to his bedroom window on the other side of the
house, and which will be discussed in the next chapter. Trees
provide welcome shade, of course, in the hot summers of south-west
France. In order to appreciate fully Louis's references to temperature, one has to imagine oneself in a climate with very hot summers
when those who can afford it do not venture out of doors unneces-
sarily during the heat of the day. This is why it is usually in the
evening that we see the family sitting outside on the terrace. Louis,
however, with his usual contradictory spirit, takes pleasure in the
midday heat, as does Marinette: 'après le déjeuner, en dépit de la
chaleur, je quittais la maison obscure et glaciale où la famille
somnolait, répandue sur les divans de cuir et sur les chaises de
paille' (p.106). With Marinette he leans his elbows on the parapet
and gazes out over the plain of the Garonne, totally deserted at this
time: 'Pas un homme, pas une bête ne sortirait avant la quatrième
heure' (p.106).

Extreme heat is often used in *Le Nœud de vipères* as a symbol
of Louis's personal agony. Apart from the night of Isa's explanation
about Rodolphe, there is the 'journée terrible dans un Bordeaux
étouffant et désert' (p.95) which Louis spends in town to avoid
keeping the promise he had unwittingly made to Marie that he
would go to hear his wife sing at mass. Here, Mauriac offers us the
classic French middle-class view of the city in August: all those who
can afford it have gone on holiday. It is 15th August, incidentally,
the feast of the Virgin Mary, and therefore his daughter's *fête*. Quite

apart from the heat of summer, Mauriac is once again using an important Christian festival as a landmark in Louis's existence.

The death of Marie herself, one of the tragedies of Louis's life, also occurs at a time of unbearable, stifling heat: 'Cet été implacable! le délire de cet été.' Louis, not given to tenderness, recollects how he had sat by Marie's bedside day after day: 'J'essuyais, pendant ces après-midi sans fin, sa petite figure qui attirait les mouches' (p.112). The cool of the evening, on the other hand, is often a time for happiness, reflection, and peace. One of Louis's happiest memories of Isa was the evening in Luchon she had burst into tears, which he had interpreted as being 'larmes de l'amour heureux' (p.58).

It is in the evening, too, that the scents of nature are particularly prominent in Louis's memories, especially where Isa is concerned: 'L'humide et tiède nuit pyrénéenne, qui sentait les herbages mouillés et la menthe, avait pris aussi de ton odeur,' he recollects (p.58). The dampness of the grass and leaves is associated with Isa's wet cheeks, still memorable to her husband years later: 'Je me rappelle l'odeur de tes joues mouillées, l'odeur de ce chagrin inconnu' (p.57). Louis also specifically remembers the 'odeur nocturne' of Isa's long dead sister Marinette (p.109), for this ability to remember a smell seems one of his most developed senses.

In a different vein, but still relating to this time of day, one of Louis's happiest memories of his little daughter Marie is the evening when she falls asleep on his lap, and he carries her up to bed, an event so rare that the family gape at him with amazement (p.95). Yet another kind of tenderness is revealed on the moonlit evening when Louis feels 'quelque douceur' in his exchanges with the abbé Ardouin (p.101).

The early morning is another time when Louis seems to be at peace with himself and the world. He greatly enjoys his early morning sorties on horseback with Marinette, who gaily puts out her tongue at Isa's shuttered window as they ride off. The abbé Ardouin, for whom Louis harbours a secret grudging respect, is always in evidence in the early morning, slipping silently off to mass before the household is awake.

This time of day holds a special charm for Louis, even in the most unlikely circumstances, such as the morning after Isa's revelations about Rodolphe. Rising early after a sleepless night, Louis is gazing alone from the terrace out over the valley to the distant village church just emerging from the mist, when he is suddenly seized with an almost religious sense of creation. From the depths of his misery, he momentarily attains a sense of spiritual security. The ever-changing face of the countryside, as we have seen already, invariably has this calming and stabilising effect on Louis's mind.

The weather, as well as the changing daily rhythms of nature, is closely linked with Louis's emotions. Rain, and in particular the dreaded hail, seem to have a surprisingly invigorating effect on him. On the night of the summer hailstorm, when he ends by considering making his peace with Isa, he leans on the window-sill contemplating the temporary lull in the storm, with the 'vent furieux' which had minutes before been raging around the house gone from his heart as well. When suddenly the storm breaks, it has an almost physical effect on him: 'ces lourdes gouttes glacées... claquaient sur les tuiles au point que j'ai eu peur de la grêle; j'ai cru que mon cœur s'arrêtait' (p.126).

Even in old age, Louis retains a surprising sensitivity to the weather. The last weeks of his life are a time of constant rain, when even Calèse seems to lose some of its charm. 'Dehors, la pluie mêle les feuilles à la boue, les pourrit,' notes Louis — an image of substances rotting in the earth which possibly prefigures his own death. Even the bushes in the garden are personalised as denuded beings exposed mercilessly to the downpour: 'Les carcasses des charmilles, les bosquets maigres grelottent sous la pluie éternelle', while the estate workers drape sacks over their heads as protection. Even indoors it is damp, so much so that Louis and his granddaughter Janine remain huddled over the fire in the sitting room until after midnight, unwilling to go upstairs to 'l'humidité pénétrante des chambres' (p.204).

The miserable weather is paralleled by the depression which Janine is suffering from after being deserted by her husband. She is suffering from delusions of persecution no less persistent than the rain, and which the family blame on Louis, although in fact, he tells us, 'au cours des interminables journées de Calèse, je lutte pied à pied contre ses illusions et ses chimères' (p.204).

Rain can of course be seen as having another significance, that of purification and cleansing, and this fits in very well with what is happening to Louis. At a time when he is thinking about the implications of taking Holy Communion again, the rain offers a form of spiritual baptism, just as in caring for Janine at her time of need, Louis has the chance to practise his new found love of others.

Thus it can be seen that Mauriac's references to the landscape, to weather and to nature are not gratuitous: the reader who pays careful attention to them will have a better understanding of the characters and their state of mind. The geographical setting, the rhythm of the seasons, the manifestations of nature which are beyond the control of man, these are used by the novelist in *Le Nœud de vipères* as the background for Louis's evolution and transformation.

3. Imagery

This chapter looks at some of the images used in *Le Nœud de vipères*, including the very important image of the title itself. Mauriac's images and symbols are always deliberately chosen to enhance our understanding of the narrative: as Bernard Chochon says in his excellent essay on *Le Nœud de vipères*, 'qu'il soit gestuel, olfactif, visuel ou auditif, le signifiant mauriacien se reconnaît toujours à sa fonction de *révélateur*. Révélateur de l'homme de Mauriac à lui-même dans l'inlassable quête de son être profond, de son moi authentique' (*8*, p.22). Whilst this chapter does not attempt to categorise exhaustively the multifaceted meanings and implications of all of these symbols, it aims, through examples, to enable readers of Mauriac's novel to formulate their own understanding of how they are used by the author.

i) Images and Symbols

The last chapter mentioned the symbolic use made of the weather to mirror and intensify emotional states, but there are other such usages. On even a fairly hasty reading of *Le Nœud de vipères*, for example, it is clear that lime trees are one very important recurring image. This is one example of how the author can influence his reader's perceptions by symbolic use of a particular theme. Mauriac uses the repeated motif of the limes, and their fragrance, just as in a piece of music a composer uses a repeated musical theme to represent a complex set of ideas which are developed throughout a composition.

Lime trees are closely associated with Louis's relationship with Isa, and his desire for human love. They appear at several memorable points in the novel, such as the warm summer's evening in Luchon when Louis sits close to Isa on a bench overlooking the town, blissfully happy and believing Isa to be so too: 'Sur la place des Thermes, que nous dominions, les feuilles des tilleuls autour du kiosque à musique étaient éclairées par les réverbères' (p.58).

These illuminated lime leaves remain fixed in Louis's memory, as does the distinctive smell of the limes. For the rest of his life, he tells us, 'Les tilleuls des allées d'Etigny, c'est toujours leur odeur que je sens, après tant d'années, quand les tilleuls fleurissent' (p.53). There is clearly some poetic licence here on Mauriac's part, since it is August when Louis meets Isa in Luchon, and the limes would have long finished flowering. Not only that, but the trees which line the Allées d'Etigny in Luchon are not limes, although there are indeed some around the bandstand on the Place des Thermes. Partly of course, this is just because Mauriac is using rather hazy memories of Luchon (his family had gone on a holiday in the Pyrenees when he was about twelve, a rare event because, as in Louis's family in the novel, it was customary for them to spend the holidays on their country estate).

But it also tells us that Mauriac particularly wanted to associate limes with Louis and Isa, especially with their happiness as a young couple. Helena Shillony, who has examined other references to lime trees in Mauriac's work, suggests that the lime is for him 'l'arbre du désir' (*23*, pp.108–10). In the context of *Le Nœud de vipères* alone, however, this is probably going too far. The rustling of the lime leaves on the night of Isa's 'confession' is indeed likened to the breathing of an invisible third person, suggesting how the unseen Rodolphe will be ever present in the couple's relationship from now on, at least for Louis. Elsewhere in the novel, however, limes spell happiness and peace, as for instance on the moonlit evening when Louis hears the abbé Ardouin utter the astounding words 'Vous êtes très bon'. Here, the pleasure Louis feels is linked inextricably to the setting: 'Nous marchions sous les tilleuls. Que tu aurais été étonnée si je t'avais dit que je trouvais quelque douceur à la présence de cet homme en soutane!' (p.101).

Walking up and down among the lime trees is where Louis seems to have most of his conversations at Calèse. On the last day he sees Isa alive, first of all he spends almost three quarters of an hour walking up and down under the limes with Bourru, the lawyer over whom he has a secret hold. Then, his plans settled, he announces his impending departure for Paris, which prompts Isa to tackle him privately, once again under the lime trees: 'Je me raccrochai un instant à son bras. Nous avions l'air, au milieu de l'allée des tilleuls, de deux époux qui finissent de vivre après des années de profonde union' (p.146).

For Louis, the worn-out old woman is still the Isa of his betrothal days, 'Isa Fondaudège, la jeune fille odorante des nuits de Bagnères' (p.147). For a moment Louis softens, and he wonders whether he has misjudged her, but the feeling passes and they walk slowly back up to the house, following not the direct route which is too steep for Louis, but taking 'l'allée des tilleuls qui contourne la maison... [qui] débouche devant la maison, du côté du Nord' (pp.149–50). It is in this same avenue of limes that Louis remembers little Marie falling and being comforted by him — a rare moment of tenderness (p.110).

When Isa dies, the limes, symbol of potential happiness, die with her. When Louis enters her empty room, from the open window he sees the limes, but uses a strange metaphor to describe them: 'Les tilleuls épais et ronds ressemblaient à des fruits touchés' _ they are like bruised fruit (p.188). That evening, after discovering Isa's letters from her confessor, Louis wanders alone and sad through the house so full of memories, feeling he can never make a fresh start: 'On ne remonte pas un tel courant de boue' (p.195), a reference to mud which reminds the reader of an earlier scene which will be discussed shortly. His children have not arrived for dinner as expected, and his efforts to talk to the servants about their daughter have been a shameful failure.

Outside, the limes are still there, but they can bring no hope to Louis now: 'Le vent tournait autour de la maison, brassait les feuilles mortes des tilleuls' (p.196). Louis will not live to see another spring and new leaves on the limes: for him, like Isa, they are dead. Lime trees are thus one of the major leitmotifs of *Le Nœud de vipères*, spanning Louis's marriage from start to finish, and marking out symbolically the major stages of its development.

Whilst on the subject of trees, we might note in passing that pine trees, often a recurring motif in Mauriac, play little part in *Le Nœud de vipères*. The nearest pine woods, where Louis and Marinette go riding together, are two kilometres away from Calèse and they have to walk their horses along the road to get there, with vineyards on either side (p.104). This corresponds to the situation of Mauriac's Malagar estate, discussed in the last chapter. Apart from this, pines feature only as a source of income: Louis knows that when his children or grandchildren need money, Isa will suggest cutting down some of the five thousand acres of pine forest he had inherited (p.52).

Some of the other motifs and symbols in the novel are also aspects of Louis's natural surroundings, for instance the vines, the weather, the temperature, or the view from Calèse, and as such are discussed in Chapter Two. As well as symbolic usages, Mauriac also employs more straightforward techniques like metaphor and simile to enhance understanding of his characters. In a first person narrative like *Le Nœud de vipères*, these techniques are of course primarily visible in the language of the narrator, and the images he uses to convey his feelings. Louis's feelings are often very strong, and the imagery he uses is correspondingly powerful.

When Louis recollects, for example, how the name of Rodolphe had wrecked his hitherto happy married life, he describes it as if it represented some dreadful scandal in Isa's past: 'Je laissais ce prénom éclater comme une bulle à la surface de notre vie. Ce qui dormait sous les eaux endormies, ce principe de corruption, ce secret putride, je ne fis rien pour l'arracher à la vase' (p.68). These are strong words to describe a perfectly innocent relationship between a well brought up young lady and a prospective suitor. The image of a 'secret putride' buried in the slime at the bottom of a pond reflects the extent of Louis's over-reaction, not the facts.

The way he disposes, next morning, of the handkerchief he had used to wipe Isa's tears away in Luchon reinforces the image of corruption. Louis had kept the handkerchief locked away in his desk, but now, dramatically, he casts it into a pond, weighted down with a stone, to bury it in the depths of mud whence he feels Isa's murky secret has risen.

It is characteristic of Louis to over-dramatise Isa's remark. In his narrative, he succeeds in creating a very dramatic picture of his fairly uneventful married life. One way he does this is by involving the reader in his battles by constant use of military language. Right at the start, when Louis recollects the scheme of vengeance he had planned years before, he refers to it as 'cette bombe à retardement' (p.37). Throughout his married life he has seen himself as waging war with his wife, and he persuades us of this by the terminology he uses to refer to their life together. 'Tu étais mon ennemie et mes enfants sont passés à l'ennemi. C'est à cette guerre qu'il faut en venir maintenant,' he writes at the end of Chapter VI (p.87).

In front of the children, he and his wife had only 'un petit nombre d'éclats terribles, où je fus le plus souvent battu'. Thereafter Louis would conduct clandestine warfare for a while: 'Après chaque défaite, une guerre souterraine se poursuivait' (p.91). The following paragraph continues the vocabulary of fighting: 'J'avais été battu (...) J'avais cédé (...) Enfin, je te forçais à en venir aux mains' (pp.91–92).

In fact, military allusions pervade Louis's *récit*. 'Battre en retraite', 'accepter le combat', the family's 'conseil de guerre', all these are expressions which stress Louis's constant battle. Such vocabulary serves to underline Louis's bitterness — how many grandfathers would look at where their family had been sitting, and think, as does Louis: 'L'ennemi avait campé là, cette nuit; il avait tenu conseil sous les étoiles' (p.150)? Even Hubert accepts that the terminology of war is appropriate, talking of 'cette triste guerre' and 'l'agresseur' (p.181) once his father has made his peace with the family.

Animal imagery is also frequently used in *Le Nœud de vipères*. When Louis is not thinking of his family as enemies, he sees them as hunters, waiting to get their quarry: 'je suis un vieillard près de mourir, au milieu d'une famille aux aguets, qui attend le moment de la curée' (p.58). He is sure that after his death they will fight 'comme des chiens' over what he leaves, and when they are all assembled on Easter Sunday, he sees them as a pack of hounds waiting for the kill: 'j'ai revu, au complet, cette meute familiale assise en rond devant la porte et m'épiant' (p.86).

Phili, the worthless husband of Louis's granddaughter Janine, is referred to as 'un vrai chien' (p.78). Phili too is waiting for Louis's death, impatient for his wife to inherit her promised fortune: 'Comme un chat entre silencieusement par la fenêtre, il a pénétré à pas de velours dans ma maison, attiré par l'odeur' (p.80). This last simile is particularly apt for the young man who tiptoes across the room while Louis appears to be asleep, and feels in his jacket for his wallet. Already, on this occasion, Louis has seen in Phili the likeness of a wolf, watching, waiting for the moment to move in on his victim: 'Je le voyais dans la pénombre, les oreilles droites. Ses yeux de jeune loup luisaient' (p.118).

The aspects of the animal kingdom invoked vary according to Louis's attitude to the person concerned. Louis has a grudging admiration, despite himself, for Phili's self-confidence and his success with women, and the images chosen suggest someone out to get what he wants.

His illegitimate son, Robert, on the other hand, is a born victim, presenting no threat to Louis, who looks forward to playing cat and mouse with him, 'à jouer comme un chat, avec ce triste mulot' (p.163). When confronting Robert with his dishonesty, Louis uses a prolonged image of someone crushing an insect. Robert is a mere 'larve', to be dealt with summarily 'comme on achève une bête', for example by crushing underfoot: 'comme... appuyer le talon sur le mille-pattes' (pp.166–67). He too is briefly likened to a dog, but to a dog who has lost a fight: 'L'échine de biais, les oreilles aplaties, il emportait, en rampant, l'os que je lui jetais' (p.168).

Those whom Louis loves are described quite differently. Luc too is an energetic hunter — indeed, Louis can even see a resemblance between him and Phili (p.119) — but he is portrayed as a part of the great outdoors he loves so much. His patience and stillness while fishing make Louis describe him as a motionless willow-tree. His presence is strangely lacking in substance: 'Il quittait le pays, en octobre, avec les autres oiseaux' (p.121), a reference to the fact that Louis only sees him during the long summer holidays.

Louis's favourite daughter Marie too is likened to a bird, an image which underlines her fragility. When Louis hugs her, he recalls that 'J'entendais battre son cœur d'oiseau. A peine lâchée, elle s'envolait dans le jardin... Marie!' (p.91). The image is apt, for neither Luc nor Marie is part of Louis's life for long, and he is powerless to protect them and keep them around him.

It is the bird image which comes to Louis's mind as he delights in his little great-granddaughter sitting on his knee in his last weeks: 'Je retrouvais, dans ses cheveux, l'odeur d'oiseau, de nid, qui me rappelait Marie (...) j'appelais dans mon cœur mon enfant perdue.' The little girl also reminds him of his nephew: 'sa chair avait le goût salé des joues de Luc' (p.206).

Some of the images operate on more than one level, adding to their impact. Louis is, for instance, constantly thirsty in the practical sense just as in the metaphysical: 'J'ai soif, et je n'ai que l'eau tiède du cabinet de toilette. Des millions, mais pas un verre d'eau fraîche' (p.119). The image of a spring of water is used to describe the type of spiritual refreshment that he finds in both Luc and Marie; in Luc, 'C'était notre Marie qui revivait pour moi, ou plutôt, la même source qui avait jailli en elle et qui était rentrée sous terre en même temps qu'elle, de nouveau sourdait à mes pieds' (p.122). Louis thinks he thirsts after money, but he is wrong: his thirst can only be satisfied when his hatred turns to love, love of the pure and selfless kind he has experienced through Marie and Luc.

The theme of choking or suffocating is another which operates on both the figurative and physical levels. The same verb *étouffer* is used to refer to the emotional effect that the 'vipers' of the title — of which more shortly — have on Louis's heart, and to the attacks of angina he suffers from. 'Un poids énorme m'*étouffait*; et, en dépit de ces *étouffements*, je ne mourais pas,' he tells us when he suffers a particularly bad attack in Paris (p.157, my italics). The physical sensation, ironically, is very similar to the emotional sickness Louis has had for years.

Perhaps more surprisingly, the same verb *étouffer* is used to describe the overwhelming sensation of love to which Louis eventually succumbs. In the very last sentence Louis writes, 'Ce qui m'*étouffe*, ce soir, en même temps que j'écris ces lignes, ce qui fait mal à mon cœur comme s'il allait se rompre cet amour dont je connais enfin le nom ador...' (p.208, my italics), the physical and emotional aspects at last become one. To the dying man, the intense physical pain in his chest is experienced as if he were being smothered by love. In this way, the image of the heart and the multiple meanings of the verb *étouffer* remain central to the novel to the end.

It is not only hatred, of course, which has been weighing heavily on Louis. In the course of the novel he frees himself from another obsession, money, and Mauriac uses the same images of crushing, strangulation, and even another snake to indicate the effect of money on Louis. When Luc goes off to war Louis offers him a money-belt which he has had specially made. He climbs on a stool to fill it with the *louis d'or* — the very name of these twenty-franc pieces is a pun on Louis and his love of gold — which he keeps hidden in a plaster bust on top of his bookshelves. As he climbs down again, particular mention is made of how heavy the belt feels around his neck: 'Ce boa engourdi, gorgé de métal, s'enroulait autour de mon cou, écrasait ma nuque' (p.124). Louis is indeed almost strangled by his greed: he says himself that this secret hoard of gold was 'ce à quoi je tenais le plus au monde' (p.124), a frightening admission.

We might see in this love of money a biblical allusion, in that Louis has to detach himself from his wealth before he is able to experience the peace of mind and the love he seeks. Yet there is no explicit reference to the words of Christ about the rich man, nor does Mauriac normally avail himself of the plentiful treasures of religious and biblical imagery which one might expect a Catholic author to draw upon in such a book. With imagination, the reader may suggest possible allusions: the vipers of the title may be linked with the serpent of the Garden of Eden, or the use of the names Marie and Luc (with the extension to Marie-Louise, or the diminutive Marinette) may be pointers on the road to redemption. While there is undoubtedly some use of such imagery, it is nonetheless true to say that most of the symbols and images in *Le Nœud de vipères* are taken from the natural world.

ii) The Title 'Le Nœud de vipères'

No discussion of imagery in *Le Nœud de vipères* would be complete without some examination of the title. Clearly, the choice of such an unusual image for a title is designed to catch the reader's attention even before he opens the book.

What are we to make of the title *Le Nœud de vipères*? Originally, Mauriac planned to call the novel *Le Crocodile* (see 2, t.II, p.1160), a less ambiguous and less evocative title, but one which would certainly have conveyed something of what Louis's family feel for him. Indeed it is a title which Louis hears applied to himself with some satisfaction. He enjoys revealing to his daughter that he knows of the nickname of 'le vieux crocodile' given to him by her irreverent son-in-law Phili, and much to her dismay, dwells on it with apparent relish: 'Crocodile je suis, crocodile je resterai. Il n'y a rien à attendre d'un vieux crocodile, rien — que sa mort' (p.79).

Mauriac may have realised the truth of this last statement. By the time the book was finished, 'crocodile' would have been a much less appropriate term for the new Louis, who sees the period after his wife's death no longer as part of his wait for death, but as the start of a new existence. Accordingly, the title was changed to *Le Nœud de vipères* by early October 1931. Mauriac had been writing the book, with interruptions, since February, and completed it in November that year. As late as 13 August, he told his teenage son Claude, 'J'appellerai mon prochain livre: *Le Crocodile*' (see 33, pp.24–25). This would have been before Chapter XVII, the dramatic chapter of Isa's death, was completed. Mauriac wrote his books fairly fast, and let them develop as they went along. It seems that he may originally have intended that the novel should finish with Isa's death. Once he had decided to show that even an old man like Louis could have a total change of heart, and feel the better for it, he proceeded to write the last three chapters, discarding the original title of *Le Crocodile* for the more enigmatic *Le Nœud de vipères*.

So ambiguous is this 'knot of vipers' that it is given different definitions in the course of the novel, each fresh definition marking a development in Louis's perception of himself and his life. In the end, the *nœud de vipères* is finally cast aside as Louis is liberated from his hatred. Such a powerful image deserves careful examination. It should be noted, first of all, that the image does not appear in the first half of the book — in other words, when Louis is still obsessed with his hatred and desire for revenge. It appears for the first time in the last chapter of Part I, when it seems Louis is near to resolving his conflicts. This is significant, since as we shall see, the vipers image is closely related to Louis's progress towards self-knowledge. Most readers quickly seize on this first mention of the title, and are content to define the knot of vipers as representing Louis's embittered heart. But this is not quite true. The first use of the image occurs, certainly, at a moment of self-examination, when Louis is stressing that he is not trying to make himself out to be better than he really is: 'Oh! ne crois pas surtout que je me fasse de moi-même une idée trop haute. Je connais mon cœur, *ce nœud de vipères*: étouffé sous elles, saturé de leur venin, il continue de battre au-dessous de ce grouillement' (p.127; the italics are mine, as in the following references to the title phrase).

Louis's heart is smothered by the vipers, poisoned by them, he acknowledges — but it is a separate entity, 'il continue de battre', a vital point, since in the end the vipers will be removed and his heart will be once more worthy of the name. Already here, in the middle of the summer night in which he has been thinking wistfully of the possibility of the love of God, Louis knows that he alone can do nothing to untangle the vipers, that only a strong external force will suffice. He continues: '*Ce nœud de vipères* qu'il est impossible de dénouer, qu'il faudrait trancher d'un coup de couteau, d'un coup de glaive: *Je ne suis pas venu apporter la paix mais le glaive*' (p.127).

Mauriac's careful build-up to Louis's 'conversion' will be discussed in Chapter Four, but let it be noted in passing that Louis's

quoting of the words of Christ in Matthew 10.34 is all the more
striking for its unexpectedness. Already, it would seem, Louis has
some strange consciousness that he can be saved from his hatred, by
a facet of God's love which would surprise his superficially religious
family as much as Christ's words did his uncomprehending
disciples.

The idea of cutting a difficult knot with a sword also reminds
us of the Gordian knot of Greek legend, of which it was said that the
person who could undo it would conquer all Asia. Severed with a
sword by Alexander the Great, it was used symbolically thereafter to
designate any very complicated problem. Louis will indeed solve his
problem, in a way which to those who know him seems no less
unexpected.

The image of cutting right through the vipers reappears
towards the end of the novel, in Chapter XVIII, when on the day
following his final return to Calèse Louis wanders through the
vineyards in a bemused state of mind, half shattered by the discovery that Isa had perhaps cared for him after all. As the rays of the
setting sun are filtered through the evening haze, Louis has a
moment of supreme truth:

> Je sentais, je voyais, je touchais mon crime. Il ne tenait
> pas tout entier dans *ce hideux nid de vipères*: haine de
> mes enfants, désir de vengeance, amour de l'argent;
> mais dans mon refus de chercher au-delà de *ces vipères
> emmêlées*. Je m'en étais tenu à *ce nœud immonde*
> comme s'il eût été mon cœur même, — comme si les
> battements de ce cœur s'étaient confondus avec ces
> reptiles grouillants. (p.191)

Here, he realises that the bitterness and hatred of the 'nœud
immonde' was not synonymous with his heart, and that he could
have overcome these evil tendencies within him. His error —
indeed, he calls it a crime — had been not to look beyond these
tendencies, not to search for his true self. With other people, too, he
had been guilty of the same crime, of not seeking to penetrate

behind their outer imperfections, and he longs to make amends towards his children. Louis is confident — wrongly, as it turns out — that this will present no problem, since the barrier on his side has been broken down at last: '*Le nœud de vipères* était enfin tranché: j'avancerais si vite dans leur amour qu'ils pleureraient en me fermant les yeux' (p.192).

This realisation, that '*le nœud de vipères* était enfin tranché', is crucial to Louis's development in the last few weeks of his life. With the barriers of hatred, avarice, vengeance and mistrust no longer separating him from his fellow men, Louis has a peace of mind never known before. While it is not made clear exactly how the knot of vipers has been cut, Louis's sudden lucidity is a major step on the path of self-knowledge which, Mauriac will imply, is also the path to grace. The reader who recollects the New Testament quotation used in Chapter XI, in the context of the sword which would be needed to cut the knot, will perceive Mauriac's unstated suggestion that Louis has been touched by divine grace.

It is these two uses of the title image, in Chapters XI and XVIII, which I believe offer the meaning that Mauriac intended by his choice of *Le Nœud de vipères* as title. Louis uses the theme on two other occasions in the novel, but at moments of bitterness when he is less lucid. Thus, at the end of Chapter XIII, after his conversation in the garden with Isa, when his heart has almost melted towards her, the sight of the circle of chairs in the garden, where his family had been plotting against him the night before, is enough to fill him with misery and hatred: 'Dans un soir d'humilité, j'ai comparé mon cœur à *un nœud de vipères*. Non, non: *le nœud de vipères* est en dehors de moi; elles sont sorties de moi et elles s'enroulaient, cette nuit, elles formaient ce cercle hideux au bas du perron, et la terre porte encore leurs traces' (p.150).

Incidentally, we might note here that 'ce cercle hideux' is just one of a series of references to circular images of various kinds which evoke unpleasant sensations for Louis: here, the circle is explicitly linked to the metaphorical vipers of the title, while elsewhere there are obvious parallels with Louis's very real suffocating fits. When Louis climbs down off the stool with the money-belt for

Luc around his neck, for example, it too is described as a reptile almost strangling him, as we have just noted, for Louis's love of money too is crushing his real self.

To return to the title, however, the image of the vipers representing his scheming family is repeated in Chapter XV, when Louis is filled with a sense of power as he accidentally discovers his son and son-in-law plotting with his illegitimate son in the church of Saint Germain-des-Prés in Paris: 'Je me sentis comme un dieu, prêt à briser ces frêles insectes dans ma main puissante, à écraser du talon *ces vipères emmêlées*, et je riais' (p.160). Here, incidentally, the mention of vipers being crushed underfoot reminds us that in Mauriac's part of the world it was not uncommon to come across a viper while out in the countryside, and that a viper's venom is poisonous. In this respect, then, the vipers' image is intimately linked to Louis's — and Mauriac's — knowledge of the countryside.

The reader may well also perceive in 'nœud de vipères' an allusion to 'nid de vipères', which adds a further dimension to the title, although it appears only once in the book (see p.191, quoted above). Such an allusion was in fact made by Mauriac himself in 1937 when explaining why he had written his next novel, *Le Mystère Frontenac*, designed to show a loving and united family: 'J'avais fait vœu...d'en écrire un [livre] qui serait *le Nid de colombes*, qui effacerait l'impression pénible laissée par le précédent' (*4*, p.112). Clearly, then, Louis's family may be seen as a *nest* of vipers in addition to the other implications.

With such a wealth of allusion, and whether 'nœud de vipères' is used to refer to the turmoil of hatred within Louis himself, or to the secret intrigues of his relatives, it is undoubtedly a powerful and expressive image which helps to portray the unpleasant and seemingly inextricable tangle that is Louis's marriage and family life. In the long run, however, Louis will no longer see his grasping family in this light, and will forgive them their machinations. Ultimately, he realises, it is not the family around him who are the vipers — despite their many failings — but the poisonous tendencies of his own heart. It is these tendencies, not his children which Louis must finally defeat and overcome. Unlike *Le Crocodile*, *Le Nœud de vipères* is a title which stresses Louis's internal conflict and development, rather than the view others have of him. The title of *Le Nœud de vipères* is a good one, for it encapsulates the very matter of the novel.

4. Louis: Conversion or Evolution?

Any discussion of *Le Nœud de vipères* would be incomplete without some attempt to analyse the metamorphosis that Louis undergoes in the course of the novel. It is true that *Le Nœud de vipères* has been described as 'la réussite accomplie d'un grand roman catholique' (*11*, p.29), but not everyone would agree. Although Mauriac himself disliked being categorised as a Catholic novelist, it seems he found the label 'catholique' acceptable for *Le Nœud de vipères*, since some twenty years later, when writing a preface to a collected edition of his works, he singled this particular book out as one of the three novels which he claimed were 'les seuls de mes romans qui méritent, sans restriction, d'être appelés catholiques — les seuls qui soient tout entiers fondés sur la Révélation' (2, t.II, p.883; the other two novels were the less well known *Les Anges noirs* and *Ce qui était perdu*).

At the same time, however, it must be realised that Mauriac was not completely satisfied with *Le Nœud de vipères*, since he hastened to write another novel, *Le Mystère Frontenac*, as an antidote to it, explaining 'Si j'avais dû mourir,' — a reference to the serious illness he suffered from shortly after *Le Nœud de vipères* was published — 'je n'aurais pas voulu que *Le Nœud de vipères* fût le dernier de mes livres' (2, t.II, p.886). Although of course we can only guess at Mauriac's reasons — and the unhappy, divided family depicted may well be one of them, since he was very touched by the love and devotion shown to him by his own family during his illness — it seems unlikely that Mauriac himself believed at the time that he had written 'un grand roman catholique', or he would surely have been less concerned about it being his last work. He was also conscious that it was very critical of the *bien-pensant* Catholic society he saw around him. Indeed, again some twenty years after the novel was written, he declared its 'thème essentiel' to be false

Christianity, 'le scandale de cet accaparement du Christ par ceux qui ne sont pas de son esprit' (2, t.II, p.885).

If we put a 'Catholic' interpretation on the novel, then we are likely to assume that Louis, the confirmed atheist, has undergone a religious conversion by the end of the novel, and become a Christian. Yet this is never explicitly stated, and indeed there is no proof that such a transformation has taken place, as Hubert's scepticism in his letter to Geneviève makes clear. All we actually know from Louis's own pen is that he becomes progressively happier towards the end of his life, and that the last words he writes suggest very strongly that he has discovered the love of God, 'cet amour dont je connais enfin le nom ador...' (p.208). While Louis is never more explicit than this, Mauriac through Janine's letter tells us of Louis's interviews with the local priest and his desire to take Holy Communion, which makes it clear that Mauriac intended a reconciliation with God.

As there is no reason to disbelieve Janine's report, it would seem reasonable to assume that Louis has undergone a complete religious transformation, and that this is the climax Mauriac intended for the novel. Mauriac himself spoke little of the nature of what happens to Louis — indeed, to have done so would undoubtedly have spoiled the deliberate imprecision of the novel's conclusion — but he did comment some twenty years later, with respect to *Le Nœud de vipères*, that 'mes monstres "cherchent Dieu en gémissant", ce que ne font presque jamais les monstres au milieu desquels nous vivons, les monstres que nous sommes nous-mêmes' (2, t.II, pp.884–85). This is very similar to the view Mauriac expressed in the foreword he wrote for *Le Nœud de vipères* when it was first published in 1932, where Louis, 'ce cœur dévoré par la haine et par l'avarice', is commended by Mauriac to the reader in the strongest possible terms: 'je veux qu'en dépit de sa bassesse vous le preniez en pitié; je veux qu'il intéresse votre cœur' (p.35). Here, Mauriac directs us straight to the novel's conclusion as the definitive answer to any questions about Louis: 'Non, ce n'était pas l'argent que cet avare chérissait, ce n'était pas de vengeance que ce furieux avait faim. L'objet véritable de son amour, vous le connaîtrez si vous avez la force et le courage d'entendre cet homme jusqu'au dernier aveu que la mort interrompt...' (p.35).

Some background information about the actual writing of *Le Nœud de vipères* may help us to understand Mauriac's intentions. In Mauriac's manuscript, the first seventeen chapters of the novel as we know it are all contained in one *cahier*, or notebook, written without any chapter divisions between February and August 1931. This part ends with the long Chapter XVII, dealing with Isa's death and its shattering effect on Louis.

The remaining three short chapters which complete Louis's narrative, and show us a transformed Louis spending the last autumn of his life at peace at his beloved Calèse, were written in a separate *cahier* in October and November that year. This suggests a certain amount of reflection on Mauriac's part before he felt sure that he should indeed continue the novel beyond Isa's death and Louis's decision to hand over his fortune to his children. Certainly, Chapter XVII offers a conclusion to the tale of Louis the grasping miser. Mauriac's decision around this time to abandon his original title of *Le Crocodile*, as mentioned in my last chapter, confirms that his plans for Louis were changing.

What would the reader have missed if the last three chapters had not been added? The answer to this question allows us to see what Mauriac wished us to feel about Louis — that the change in him was far more profound than merely a new unselfish attitude to his wealth.

The chronology of the narrative, too, confirms that Mauriac intended what happens to Louis in the course of the book to be seen as a form of religious conversion. The entire text can be clearly dated as it is written by Louis, between Easter and November during a year in the 1930s, in fact probably in 1930 (see *27*, pp.90–91, and *23*, p.76), the year before Mauriac wrote the novel. What better moment of the religious calendar could Mauriac have chosen, for the start of Louis's self-exploratory confession, than the traditional paschal season of repentance and redemption?

Initially, Louis's only interest in Easter is the opportunity it affords him to flout his wife's religious principles, by eating meat on Easter Friday, while the rest of the family abide by the Catholic practice of eating fish. All four generations of the family, from Louis down to his great-granddaughter, are at Calèse, but Louis feels even more isolated than usual: 'Dans la nuit de Pâques, la maison est chargée de couples. Et moi, je pourrais être le tronc vivant de ces jeunes rameaux. La plupart des pères sont aimés' (p.87). Louis's loneliness makes him reflect on the void of death, which to him seems all the more unfair because he feels he has had so little from life: 'Vous ne pouvez imaginer ce supplice: ne rien avoir eu de la vie et ne rien attendre de la mort. Qu'il n'y ait rien au-delà du monde, qu'il n'existe pas d'explication, que le mot de l'énigme ne nous soit jamais donné...' (p.81).

The very fact that Louis sees the world as an enigma, of course, is evidence that he is far from the clear-cut atheist that he proclaims himself to be. Moreover, there is irony in the fact that it should be Louis, the staunch atheist, who meditates on the meaning of life and death at Easter, while his church-going family use the religious feast to settle financial affairs and look after family business interests. But such irony is vital to Mauriac's thesis, that those around Louis are 'chrétiens médiocres' who are useless as pointers to the path to truth, while the sinner himself struggles alone to reach it. Louis is left severely alone in the face of approaching death, which he fears so much that even to fall asleep seems to be tempting fate: 'A mon âge, le sommeil attire l'attention de la mort. Tant que je resterai debout, il me semble qu'elle ne peut pas venir.' What he fears in death is its incomprehensibility, the fact that it can only be interpreted as a blank, as the negation of existence: 'Ce que je redoute d'elle, est-ce l'angoisse physique, l'angoisse du dernier hoquet? Non, mais c'est qu'elle est ce qui n'existe pas, ce qui ne peut se traduire que par le signe —' (p.87).

As Louis's preoccupation with death leads him to ponder why everything had gone wrong in his life, references to the time of writing disappear almost completely. Chapters VI to X are devoted mainly to recollections of the past, filling in for us the major events of Louis's life since his marriage. During these reminiscences, there are no references to the act of writing them, so that there is a linger-

ing impression that time has stood still at Easter. Only in the second
last chapter of Part I of the novel do we in fact learn that Louis has
been laid low by a major seizure for a month after Easter. This
confirms that his premonition of death is not that of a mere
hypochondriac, and prepares us for his suffocating fit which opens
Chapter XI, the concluding chapter of Part I and a major turning
point in Louis's pursuit of self-knowledge.

The start of the 'Deuxième partie' after the critical night of
the summer hailstorm is not an artificial break, for it marks the start
of a transformation in Louis's character, as well as a change in his
attitude towards what he is writing. No longer is he writing with the
aim of his manuscript being read after his death, and indeed he
thinks he will destroy it as soon as he feels dangerously ill. Yet he
knows he will continue writing: 'A quoi bon reprendre ce travail?
C'est qu'à mon insu, sans doute, j'y trouvais un soulagement, une
délivrance' (p.131). The cathartic and self-exploratory function of
Louis's narrative becomes more apparent as Part II progresses.

Part II also introduces a different form of narrative structure.
Whereas Part I narrates Louis's entire life as he looks back on it,
part II is much less condensed, and deals chronologically with the
last five months of Louis's life, from July to November 1930. It is
far from being a diary, however, for at no time, except in Chapter
XIV, does Louis actually 'write up' events as they happen. A certain
distance in time seems necessary for him to analyse, digest and
recreate recent events. Thus, only in Paris does Louis finish telling
us what happened at Calèse (Chapters XII and XIII), and the bulk of
what happens in Paris is only related once he has returned to Calèse
(Chapters XV and XVI). As Jacques Petit puts it, 'Jamais le journal
ne rejoint tout à fait le présent' (see 2, t.II, p.1166). Even when in
the last chapters, we feel most closely in touch with Louis'
thoughts, it is made clear to us that there has been some considerable passage of time before the narrative that we are reading. At the
end of Chapter XIX, the reference to a letter from Geneviève
(p.202) means that the events of which we have just heard, the
aftermath of Phili's departure, had taken place more than two weeks
previously. Even the last words Louis writes, about the evening

when he had, in vain, attempted to comfort Janine as she sat by the fire, are written some time later. Only the very last sentence, unfinished, visibly refers to the actual moment of writing.

Why such a gap? Why does Mauriac not bring us up to date with Louis's thoughts? For one thing, it means we do not see the final evolution in Louis's mind. Some three or four weeks before his death, for example, he has the first of three interviews with the local priest that Janine tells us of later (p.214). Why does Louis never mention these meetings in his diary?

The answer lies in Mauriac's aims for his novel. Allowing Louis to cast a veil over the end of his life is fundamental to the way Mauriac wants the novel to conclude. The need to portray in words the conversion of a lifelong atheist is avoided, and the essentials of his death, material and spiritual, can be conveyed in the two letters which conclude the book. Hubert's letter also reinforces the impression of the family's lack of comprehension which we have received from Louis, and Mauriac thereby contrives to increase our sympathy for Louis.

Janine's letter, on the other hand, stresses the spiritual transformation which Mauriac wishes us to perceive in Louis. That Janine's letter should be Mauriac's last word is no accident: originally Mauriac had written a letter from Geneviève to follow Hubert's, full of the same stupidity and uncomprehending harshness towards their father. In the final version, however, Mauriac substituted the letter from Janine, thereby altering the conclusion from one of bitterness and family strife to a note of peace and hope.

The precise date of Louis's death is also carefully chosen by Mauriac. Louis dies in the night of 23 November, which, as John Flower has pointed out, 'is not only the eve of the feast of St John of the Cross, but also the night when two hundred and seventy-six years before Pascal too had discovered faith' (*14*, p.56). The choice of Pascal's night of revelation need not surprise us, for the great Jansenist thinker of the seventeenth century had exercised a profound influence over Mauriac ever since his schooldays, and in 1931, the year he wrote *Le Nœud de vipères*, he published a study of Pascal.

Louis's journey of self-exploration, begun at the major Christian festival of repentance and expiation, ends abruptly in what Mauriac hopes the reader will interpret as a conversion no less profound than Pascal's, in final, if unfinished, recognition of 'cet amour dont je connais enfin le nom ador...' (p.208). It ends, too, at a season when Louis is only too conscious of the approach of Advent and Christmas. From Janine's letter we learn that despite his longing to receive Communion, Louis felt himself so unworthy that he had decided to wait until Christmas: 'Oui, l'avant-veille de sa mort, le mercredi, je l'entends encore, dans le salon de Calèse, me parler de ce Noël désiré, avec une voix pleine d'angoisse' (p.215). That Louis should not live long enough to receive Communion is fully in keeping with the suggestive, rather than conclusive, ending that Mauriac wishes to give to his novel.

Such deliberate matching of dates to landmarks in Louis's development is obviously meant to underline his spiritual progress. Indeed, throughout the novel Mauriac is careful to highlight how Louis's attitudes change, as they have done in the past. Louis is not, for example, brought up with any antagonistic attitudes to religion: his mother, although not a regular churchgoer herself, has him baptised as a baby, and he made his First Communion in due course, along with his classmates, but these were mere formalities to which he gave no thought. Not until he was an undergraduate did Louis develop specifically anticlerical attitudes: 'La haine de la religion, qui a été si longtemps ma passion dominante,...prit naissance à la Faculté de Droit, en 1879 et en 1880, au moment du vote de l'article 7, l'année des fameux décrets et de l'expulsion des jésuites' (p.50). This is a reference to the legislation introduced in France at that time to weaken the traditionally strong role of Catholic religious orders, such as the Jesuits, in educating the young. Louis, educated in a state *lycée* and bitterly jealous of the social advantages he perceives in his fellow students educated in church schools, seizes the opportunity to make a political stance by developing an anti-clerical position.

It is clear that for the young Louis religion is the possession of the higher social classes, something to be rejected along with their other attributes. It is perhaps not surprising that his anti-clerical beliefs develop at the same time as a burning desire for social justice, which leads him to improve the housing conditions of tenants on the family estates. His attitude is clear when he goes to mass with Isa and her family in Luchon, describing it as 'une sorte de religion des ancêtres à l'usage de la bourgeoisie, un ensemble de rites dépourvus de toute signification autre que sociale' (p.56). This is not far removed from the attitudes of Isa's family, who do not expect a man to be interested in religion: 'Dans ton monde, un mari "accompagnait sa femme à la messe": C'était la formule reçue' (p.66). This is, of course, precisely the sort of 'show' religion which Louis comes to hate, but which is typical of his family, whom Mauriac in his foreword condemns as 'chrétiens médiocres'.

Initially, Louis's attitude is far from fixed. Indeed, it is clear that in his youth his supposed anti-clericalism is no more than skin deep. The joy he experiences with Isa makes him receptive to all kinds of new experiences, and the novel is not far advanced when the reader gets the first hint that Louis's irreligion is not as profound as he makes it out to be. Though he has never dared tell Isa, it was through her, in the blissful days of their engagement, that he had had his first taste of belief in something beyond the grave: 'J'étais un autre homme, au point qu'un jour…sur la route de la vallée du Lys, nous étions descendus de la victoria. Les eaux ruisselaient; j'écrasais du fenouil entre mes doigts; au bas des montagnes, la nuit s'accumulait, mais, sur les sommets, subsistaient des camps de lumière…J'eus soudain la sensation aiguë, la certitude presque physique *qu'il existait un autre monde*, une réalité dont nous ne connaissions que l'ombre…' (pp.58–59, my italics).

Certain features of this important moment are significant: Louis is intensely happy to be with his fiancée, and he feels in communion with nature, which assails his senses in unforgettable style. The smell and feel of the fennel he crushes between his fingers, the changing light patterns as night falls over the valley, the sound of the river below — all these form part of Louis's startling experience, which might here be more properly termed pantheistic rather than religious, were it not for the fact that Louis relates it by implication to Christian belief in an afterlife. Already here Mauriac informs us that such a moment, while infrequent, was not unique: 'Ce ne fut qu'un instant, — et qui, au long de ma triste vie, se renouvela à de très rares intervalles. Mais sa singularité même lui donne à mes yeux une valeur accrue.' That such an experience was not easily pushed aside, that it sowed in Louis the seed of doubt about his convictions, is made plain by the revealing comment which follows: 'Et c'est pourquoi, plus tard, dans le long débat religieux qui nous a déchirés, il me fallut écarter un tel souvenir...' (p.59).

Louis's background had given him so little contact with the Church that, as he readily admits, 'Mon ignorance était profonde en ces matières' (p.50). Yet, despite this, the adult Louis is well aware of the principles of Christianity. He is, for example, more conscious than his supposedly religious family of what death should mean to a Christian. When his beloved daughter Marie dies, Louis has an overwhelming sensation that the real Marie is no longer present in her physical remains, in contrast to Isa's grief-stricken reaction to the lifeless body: 'Ta foi ne te servait à rien. Tu ne pensais qu'à cette chair de ta chair qui allait être ensevelie et qui était au moment de pourrir; tandis que moi, l'incrédule, j'éprouvais devant ce qui restait de Marie, tout ce que signifie le mot "dépouille". J'avais le sentiment irrésistible d'un départ, d'une absence. Elle n'était plus là; ce n'était plus elle' (p.113). Already here we have a foretaste of the value of redemption Louis will later come to appreciate in Marie's death, as he deliberately uses the words of the angel at the empty tomb to express how he feels: 'Vous cherchez Marie? Elle n'est plus ici...' (cf. Matthew 28. 5–6).

Such a formula in the mouth of Louis may surprise the reader, but as Alexander Fischler has noted, 'Louis knows the Gospels extremely well' (*13*, p.387). While it might be argued that Louis's ability to quote the Gospels is contrived and unrealistic, Louis the lawyer would have known only too well how a successful attack depends on having the facts at one's fingertips. Either the requirements of his political activities, or the perverse pleasure he takes in upsetting Isa, might have led him to such study.

Indeed, Louis delights in pointing out to Isa how many of her actions do not conform to the standards set down by Christ. His superior skill at manipulating words means he can discomfit his wife without difficulty, while feigning innocence: ' "Tiens, disais-je, je croyais que le Christ avait dit..." ... "Il ne faut pas prendre au pied de la lettre...," balbutiais-tu. Sur quoi je triomphais aisément et t'accablais d'exemples pour te prouver que la sainteté consiste justement à suivre l'Evangile au pied de la lettre' (p.97). He had noted with some irony how his wife, while discharging what she saw as her 'devoirs envers les pauvres', had been mean and penny-pinching where her own servants were concerned: 'obtenir le plus de travail pour le moins d'argent possible' had been the rule she operated on (p.96). Interestingly, Louis notices how his wife changes in later years, doing works of a more genuinely charitable nature, though Mauriac does not develop this.

While the children were young, Louis had constantly attacked his wife's beliefs in every way he could. He had delighted in the naïve seminary student, l'abbé Ardouin, who had come as tutor to the children one summer, since it was easy to inveigle him into utterances which contradicted Isa's. The Dreyfus affair, of which the newspapers were full at the time, had offered Louis endless opportunities. Isa was not interested in the rights or wrongs of the case, but followed the right-wing anti-Semitic views of what Louis acidly describes as the 'bons journaux' (p.98), namely that even if the wrong man had been condemned, it mattered little, especially as he was a Jew, compared with the damage that a thorough investigation would cause to the French military establishment. As a true Christian, however, the abbé Ardouin was honest enough to agree with Louis that an innocent person should not be condemned.

Despite the teasing, this 23-year-old seminary student had through one small episode had an enormous influence on Louis, who recognised that, alone of all the so-called Christians around him, it was the young *abbé* who genuinely followed the precepts of Christ. 'Que tu aurais été étonnée si je t'avais dit que je trouvais quelque douceur à la présence de cet homme en soutane! C'était vrai pourtant,' Louis recollects (p.101). Grateful for Louis's dismissive attitude towards the youthful escapade which had so shocked the local *curé*, the young man utters words which to Louis are unforgettable: 'Vous êtes très bon.' Furthermore, he stoutly maintains this in the face of Louis's disbelieving laughter.

The *abbé* is just one of several innocents who are milestones on Louis's path to enlightenment, and whom we meet in succession in Chapters VII to X of the novel, before the end of Part I. True Christians, Mauriac suggests, are not necessarily those who simply perform all the required duties: an acknowledged sinner like the abbé Ardouin, who believes with his superiors that his one night at the theatre had been such a scandal that 'ce ne serait pas trop de toute sa vie pour réparer ce qu'il avait fait' (p.100), is far nearer to God than Isa with her self-righteousness. Louis knows that even at that stage in his life, he had realised the *abbé* represented true Christianity, and felt guilty for not acknowledging the fact: 'je n'avais pas une bonne conscience: je feignais de croire...qu'aucune trace de l'esprit du Christ ne subsistait plus parmi vous, et je n'ignorais pas que, sous mon toit, un homme vivait selon cet esprit, à l'insu de tous' (p.101) — that is, unknown to all but Louis.

With what is, for her, surprising perception, Isa picks out in the abbé Ardouin the quality of innocence which in *Le Nœud de vipères* seems the prerequisite for characters who affect Louis: 'C'est un saint garçon, mais un véritable enfant qui ne croit pas au mal' (p.98). The pre-adult age is frequently associated in Mauriac with purity and innocence, as for example in *Thérèse Desqueyroux*, where Thérèse contrasts the purity of her schoolgirl years with her life since marriage.

This innocence of youth is present in both Marie and Luc, in different ways. Luc, an outdoor boy who loves fishing and hunting, and is greatly amused at the way his aunt and cousins seem terrified of his uncle, is not a conventionally pious child. Indeed, Isa, who dislikes him, calls him 'une petite brute', but Louis sees beyond his careless exterior to find a 'pureté' and an 'ignorance du mal' which greatly affects him: 'La pureté, chez lui, ne semblait ni acquise ni consciente: C'était la limpidité de l'eau dans les cailloux. Elle brillait sur lui, comme la rosée dans l'herbe. Si je m'y arrête, c'est qu'elle eut en moi un retentissement profond' (p.121). Luc had shown to Louis something which Isa could never have done, 'le sens du mal', and his unaffected innocence had made Louis conscious of his own unworthiness: 'je sentais auprès de lui ma difformité' (p.121).

Luc, like the others who stand out as unconscious beacons to Louis on his path to redemption, has only a brief part to play: he comes to stay only in the summer holidays, and Louis admits he never thinks of him the rest of the year. Then, before reaching adulthood, Luc disappears on active service in 1918 in the last months of the Great War, after rejecting the one generous gift Louis had ever thought of making. But he leaves Louis a priceless keepsake, a postcard signed ' Tendresses', a word which so thrills his uncle that he keeps the postcard in his wallet for the rest of his life.

Oddly enough, Louis cannot help seeing in Luc 'le frère de la petite fille endormie douze années plus tôt', despite the fact that Luc seems the opposite of Marie in every way. Yet Louis grows to understand what the similarity is, not a surface resemblance but something more profound: 'Dans le fils de Marinette...C'était notre Marie qui revivait pour moi, ou plutôt, la même source qui avait jailli en elle et qui était rentrée sous terre en même temps qu'elle, de nouveau sourdait à mes pieds' (p.122). It had not been Marie's persistent, well-behaved piety which had affected her father, but her simple good-heartedness and generosity, together with her unrestrained affection for him. As with Luc, there was undoubtedly something of the attraction of opposites for Louis in this his youngest child, of whom it was said 'elle donnerait tout ce qu'elle a; l'argent ne lui tient pas aux doigts' (p.94). Years later, the memory of Marie's delirious cries 'pour papa! pour papa!' on her deathbed helps Louis come to his final decision: 'A ce chevet...le secret de la mort et de la vie m'a été livré...' (p.207).

The use of the death of a child, in particular a favourite daughter, as an emotional step towards a religious conversion, is of course neither subtle nor original. Indeed, the equating of the sufferings of the dying child with the agony of Christ on the cross, in Louis's assertion that 'une petite fille mourait pour moi' (p.207), may well appear somewhat contrived. Yet somehow Mauriac — for most readers — just escapes the accusation of overt manipulation. It is scarcely surprising that Louis, as he feels death approach, should look back at the major landmarks of his life, and it would be wrong to classify his reflections as the sentimental outburst of an old man no longer in full control. This would be to deny Louis the lucidity which Mauriac clearly intends him to have. This is made quite clear on the crucial night of the summer hailstorm, when Louis confesses that 'c'est lorsque je me sens le plus lucide, que la tentation chrétienne me tourmente', and that he no longer believes what he had put years before among papers to be read in the event of his death, that only if he were not in full control of his faculties would he ever accept to see a priest (pp.126–27).

Yet *Le Nœud de vipères* is not designed to show us a deathbed conversion in the usual sense of the term, but rather to highlight Louis's ever-increasing self-knowledge, which by implication leads to knowledge of the love of God. Louis dies without taking Communion, or receiving the last rites administered to the dying in the Catholic Church, both of which Mauriac could have put in if he had desired, as he does in other works.

One reason for this is that *Le Nœud de vipères* is not a book about religion, but it is concerned with what might well be termed religious experience. While we may be tempted to conclude that Louis's transformation is portrayed on a human rather than a religious plane — and it would certainly be hard to use the word 'Catholic' to describe it — it must be acknowledged that Mauriac uses the Catholic Church as his constant background standard. Nevertheless, Louis shows little interest in the practices of the Church, the attitudes of most of its members in the book are censured, and paradoxically it is the student priest condemned by the Church who aids Louis in his search. Louis seeks not the externals of religious practice (is this perhaps why Mauriac never allows him to go as far as receiving Communion?), but the fundamentals of man's existence in the world. In the end, Louis finds what he is seeking despite, rather than through, the actions of his supposedly 'religious' family.

First, though, he has to realise that practice and reality in religion may be far apart, and that his dislike of the one has led him erroneously to disregard the other: 'cette caricature grossière, cette charge médiocre de la vie chrétienne, j'avais feint d'y voir une représentation authentique pour avoir le droit de la haïr' (p.207). In the second last paragraph he writes before his death, Louis acknowledges how he has fought against salvation for years: 'Inlassablement, j'ai cherché à perdre cette clef qu'une main mystérieuse m'a toujours rendue, à chaque tournant de ma vie' (p.207). Mauriac wants us to see that it is through no act, or even merit, of Louis himself that he finds grace in the end, but rather that God — and herein lies the Christian implication of the novel — has persistently sought out the sinner until the latter can resist no longer.

The repeated 'keys' held out to Louis have been of two kinds: natural phenomena which have made a particular impression on him, and individuals whose purity and simplicity have deeply touched him. Isa, too, has had a major influence on Louis. Indeed, in a peculiar, almost paradoxical, way, Louis's progress towards belief is closely linked to Isa. It is not by chance that his first assurance of another world comes while he is with Isa, in the Lys valley at Luchon. Not long after, still stunned by Isa's revelations about Rodolphe, Louis has another strangely spiritual experience as he watches the village church gradually emerge from the morning mist: 'Un clocher naissait du brouillard, puis l'église à son tour en sortait, comme un corps vivant.' The sensation of life in the wobbly, indistinct shape of the church, leads Louis to meditate on the possibility that 'les événements, surtout dans l'ordre du cœur, sont peut-être des messagers dont il faut interpréter le secret...' In later years, even as he remembers his agony, Louis senses that he had been closer to Isa than either of them had realised: 'Oui, j'ai été capable, à certaines heures de ma vie, d'entrevoir ces choses qui auraient dû me rapprocher de toi' (p.73).

Similarly, at the end of Part I, when Louis realises his impotence in the face of the hailstorm at three o'clock in the morning, and philosophically accepts it in strangely Christian terms, saying 'je ne puis plus rien récolter au monde' (p.126), it is once again to Isa that he turns, at least on paper, though this time he goes so far as to visualise a real-life reconciliation with her. Significantly, she is the one to whom he most longs to confess his desire to believe. When in a roundabout way he explains here that he may be beginning to believe in God, he does so in a cautious statement addressed to Isa: 'Je ne puis plus nier qu'une route existe en moi qui pourrait mener à ton Dieu'. Isa, for Louis, represents much that he dislikes in the Church, yet he persists in linking her with what he feels called to seek: 'Ce n'est peut-être pas pour vous, les justes, que ton Dieu est venu, s'il est venu, mais pour nous' (p.127).

To understand the idea put forward by Louis here is vital to understanding Mauriac's aims in *Le Nœud de vipères*. Louis is undoubtedly meant to be seen as a selfish and unhappy sinner, who has caused much sorrow around him, but no one must be seen as beyond redemption. Louis, by accepting his own unworthiness, by honestly admitting the nature of 'mon cœur, ce cœur, ce nœud de vipères' (p.127), has crossed the hurdle of repentance and is ready to receive the love of God. Self-righteous Catholics, who like Janine can say 'bien sûr, je suis religieuse, je remplis mes devoirs' (p.206), but who are insensitive to the meaning of true Christian charity, are incapable of understanding the nature of sin and repentance, and thus, like Hubert, cannot understand that Louis's transformation is genuine. For Mauriac, Louis's transformation is the love of God in action, the working of God's ineffable mysteries on an embittered heart which everyone would have thought impossible to touch. In this sense, *Le Nœud de vipères* is indeed a profoundly Christian novel.

It seems to me that the secret of the success of *Le Nœud de vipères* is that Mauriac refrains from the obvious. Louis's life has been a search, and the end of the novel shows the satisfactory conclusion of that search. Louis has found what he was seeking all his life, namely love. He had met it all too briefly in his mother, in his wife, in Marie and Luc, and even in the abbé Ardouin, but never in a lasting form. Only once he is at peace with himself does he find it truly. This is the meaning of Mauriac's prefatory quotation from

St Teresa of Avila, reformulated by Louis once he hands his money over to his children: 'Nous ne savons pas ce que nous voulons, et... nous nous éloignons infiniment de ce que nous désirons' (p.34 and p.185). Louis had thought he wanted success, power, and wealth, but all these had brought him no happiness. He had thought he wanted revenge on Isa, but her death had made him realise they could have loved one another. Only when he divests himself of his fortune, and ceases to let hatred run his life, can he attain a state of peace.

In an earlier age, *Le Nœud de vipères* might have been interpreted as a morality tale, and it is undoubtedly true that Louis's tale might be held up as a warning. Yet he dies happy, feeling needed by his granddaughter and delighting in her child who reminds him of the long dead Marie. His family can see no difference in him, however: part of the function of the letters at the end of the novel is to make sure that the dénouement is anchored in reality, for Mauriac does not want to be accused of artificially contriving an unrealistic ending. Hubert's view of his father does not change, and Janine has not had the benefit of reading the manuscript to confirm her intuitive feelings. Only we, Mauriac's readers, can vouch with certainty for Louis's change of heart.

Conclusion

What did Mauriac intend us to think of Louis and of *Le Nœud de vipères* as a whole? Clearly, Louis is an unhappy and embittered old man, who has brought much of his unhappiness upon himself. His family, on the other hand, is not exactly blameless either, nor are its members models of contentment. The only true, sincere, and good characters in the novel make no more than brief appearances before they disappear for ever.

Must we then classify *Le Nœud de vipères* as a bleak and pessimistic novel, in which there is little hope of human happiness? Clearly we cannot, since whatever we make of the end of the novel, it is plain that Mauriac intends Louis's last days to show a complete change, and a peace of heart which he has never known before. 'Dans son fond,' Mauriac said of *Le Nœud de vipères* in 1933, 'c'est l'histoire d'une remontée' (*3*, p.132). Yet the novel can in no way be described as having a happy ending, for it is too late for Louis to undo what is past, or to be reconciled to Isa. In addition, the rest of the family remain set in their ways and, with the exception of Janine, are blind to any change in Louis.

Surely, then, we can conclude only that the novel is inconclusive. For the reader, this is a considerable advantage, for it leaves us free to meditate on what we feel to be the important points of the book. Pigheadedness, pride, love of money, worry about appearances, lack of communication: all these things have contributed to unhappiness on both sides of the family. Self-centredness, in the case of Louis, has undoubtedly been a major factor in making him miserable. If we wished, therefore, we could draw a Victorian-style moral conclusion. Would this be fair? Probably not. While Mauriac certainly draws our attention to the less admirable qualities in human nature, these aspects form only the background to the individual human drama which is Mauriac's central concern

How Louis develops, how his mind works, how change occurs, these are what Mauriac concentrates on. The actual processes of the human mind are central to the novel. Mauriac is more interested, I would suggest, in the gradual developments taking place in Louis's mind than in the eventual conclusion.

This is borne out by the inconclusiveness of the novel. Louis, who is clearly closest to his creator's heart, dies happy, but beyond that Mauriac is not over-concerned with the precise details of what the reader thinks. Whether Louis is 'converted' or not, is something left for the reader to decide. To me, this is part of the novel's appeal. Whether we are Christian or not, whether we believe in conversions or not, is of no consequence for our appreciation of the human drama Mauriac portrays. I stress the word 'human', for I firmly believe that human nature, and not religion, is Mauriac's central concern. In *Le Nœud de vipères* we follow Louis from childhood to death, in his continual struggle to deal with other people. Comment there is in plenty, on Louis's upbringing, on the society he lives in, but it is never direct. The reader must look carefully for it, and draw his or her own conclusions from Mauriac's remarks.

We may find this irritating, as others have done before. Catholic critics would have liked Mauriac to write a clearly Catholic novel. Others feel that the hints of conversion are so strong, although not specifically stated, that Mauriac is unfairly trying to write about a conversion while pretending he is doing no such thing — a sneaky trick which they dislike. Reading a novel is a personal and individual enterprise, and everyone's reactions are different.

Whatever we feel about the end of the novel, it cannot be denied that *Le Nœud de vipères* has moments of mastery. The portrayal of nature, the intimate relationship between Louis and the world around him, the magical rebirth of the countryside through the shimmering haze of a hot summer day dawning, the capturing of the innocence of childhood through such a detail as a little girl's dresses hanging out to dry between the apple trees, all this is part of Mauriac's skilful creation of life in a given part of France, but of life as it might be anywhere.

It is life that Mauriac is concerned with, for *Le Nœud de vipères* is a profound statement about human nature, about man's isolation and desire for contact with something or someone greater than himself. It is a bitter indictment of 'les chrétiens médiocres' mentioned by Mauriac in his foreword and whom we see all too clearly in the book. Above all, it shows us that self-knowledge is essential for mental well-being. Louis, for all his heart trouble and impending death, is mentally and spiritually fitter at the end of the book than when we first saw him. His hatred at that point had devoured him, and 'le nœud de vipères' was in control. What the novel shows us is Louis's gradual emergence from the viper's coils, to what is virtually a new life, a new existence at peace with the world and himself. His death, at this point, is immaterial, for his search is over. Whether we choose to put a Christian interpretation on the novel's ending or not is irrelevant, for Louis's transformation is complete in this world, and like the novelist we need not concern ourselves with the next.

In taking on the task of showing from the inside the way in which a sinner could be redeemed, Mauriac knew he was treading a difficult path. It was made no easier by the choice of the first person narrative, not a common feature in Mauriac's novels. To show a conversion and its consequences is hard enough; to show the actual process of conversion from within, delicately and without the appearance of firm authorial direction, is a major undertaking. That Mauriac succeeds is, I believe, largely due to his willingness to understate, to relate Louis's development almost, but not quite, exclusively to nature and to self-knowledge, to man in the world of nature around him, rather than to God and His world. It is 'the fusion of these two worlds — pagan and Christian', as John Flower puts it, which becomes for Mauriac 'the very substance of his achievement as a Catholic novelist' (*15*, p.14). Human love, divine love, and love of nature are all inextricably linked. Louis's 'signposts' on the way to redemption are not all recognisable by normal religious standards: often, they take the form of fleeting moments of happiness, of unity with nature, or oneness with creation, for this is the very essence of man's experience in the world as presented in *Le Nœud de vipères*.

Select Bibliography

A. EDITIONS USED OF WORKS BY MAURIAC

1. *Le Nœud de vipères*, edited by John T. Stoker and Robert Silhol, London, Harrap, 1959. All references to the text are to this edition, although its introduction and notes are not particularly helpful. It is, however, widely used by students, and page references remain constant in reprintings, unlike that of the other most frequently used edition, the Livre de Poche.
2. *Œuvres romanesques et théâtrales complètes*, édition établie, présentée et annotée par Jacques Petit, Bibliothèque de la Pléiade, Paris, Gallimard, t.I, 1978; t.II, 1979; t.III, 1981; t.IV, 1985. *Le Nœud de vipères* is in volume II of this excellent annotated edition, along with Mauriac's essays on *Le Roman* and *Le Romancier et ses personnages*.
3. *Le Romancier et ses personnages*, précédé d'une étude d'Edmond Jaloux, Paris, Corrêa, 1933; reprint, Editions Buchet-Chastel, 1984.
4. *Les Paroles restent*: interviews recueillies et présentées par Keith Goesch, Paris, Grasset, 1985. A useful collection of interviews given by Mauriac over the years, grouped by subject, with index.

B. BOOKS AND ARTICLES RELEVANT TO THE STUDY OF LE NŒUD DE VIPERES

Particularly relevant items are marked with an asterisk.*

5. Batchelor, R., 'Art and Theology in Mauriac's *Le Nœud de vipères*', *Nottingham French Studies*, 12 (1973), 33–43.
6. Beaumont, Ernest, 'The Supernatural in Dostoyevsky and Bernanos: A Reply to Professor Sonnenfeld', *French Studies*, 23 (1969), 261–71.
*7. Canérot, Marie-Françoise, *Mauriac après 1930: le roman dénoué*, Paris, SEDES, 1985.
*8. Chochon, Bernard, *Structures du 'Nœud de vipères' de Mauriac: une haine à entendre*, Archives des Lettres Modernes, no. 216, Paris, Minard, 1984.

9. Deam, Anne, '*La Symphonie pastorale* et *Le Nœud de vipères*: pouvoir transformateur du roman journal', *Chimères*, 13 (1980), 55–67.

10. Denommé, Robert T., '*The Viper's [sic] Tangle*: Relative and Absolute Values', *Renascence*, 18 (1965–66), 32–39.

11. Du Bos, Charles, *François Mauriac et le problème du romancier catholique*, Paris, Corrêa, 1933.

12. Dupeyron, Georges, '*Le Nœud de vipères*' [review], *Europe*, septembre 1932, reprinted in *Europe*, nos 533–34 (septembre–octobre 1973), 100–02.

13. Fischler, Alexander, 'Thematic Keys in François Mauriac's *Thérèse Desqueyroux* and *Le Nœud de vipères*' *Modern Language Quarterly*, 40 (1979), 376–89.

*14. Flower, John, *A Critical Commentary on Mauriac's 'Le Nœud de vipères'*, London: Macmillan, 1969.

*15. ——, *Intention and Achievement: An Essay on the Novels of François Mauriac*, Oxford, Clarendon Press, 1969.

16. Madaule, Jacques, 'La Grâce dans l'œuvre de François Mauriac', *Revue des Lettres Modernes*, nos 516–22 (1977), *François Mauriac* 2, 77–91.

17. Kushner, Eva, *Mauriac*, Paris, Desclée de Brouwer, Collection 'Les Ecrivains devant Dieu', 1972.

18. Maucuer, Maurice, 'La Grâce enfantine dans l'univers romanesque de François Mauriac', *Revue des Lettres Modernes*, nos 516–22 (1977), *François Mauriac* 2, pp.51–75.

19. Mein, Margaret, 'François Mauriac and Jansenism', *Modern Language Review*, 58 (1963), 516-23.

*20. Monférier, Jacques, *François Mauriac du 'Nœud de vipères' à 'La Pharisienne'*, Paris, Champion, 1985.

21. Paine, Ruth Benson, *Thematic Analysis of François Mauriac's 'Génitrix', 'Le Désert de l'amour', and 'Le Nœud de vipères'*, Mississippi, Romance Monographs, No. 20, 1976.

*22. Shillony, Helena, '*Le Nœud de vipères:* pour une définition générique', *Revue des Lettres Modernes*, nos 516–22 (1977), *François Mauriac* 2, pp.95–107.

*23. ——, *Le Roman contradictoire: une lecture du 'Nœud de vipères' de Mauriac*, Archives des Lettres Modernes, no.179 (Archives François Mauriac, 3), Paris, Minard, 1978.

24. Sonnenfeld, Albert, 'The Catholic Novelist and the Supernatural', *French Studies*, 22 (1968), 307–19.

25. Swift, Bernard C., 'Consistency in François Mauriac's *Le Nœud de vipères*', *Western Canadian Studies in Modern Languages and Literature*, 2 (1970), 44–57.

26. Prud'homme, Jeannine, 'L'expression stylistique de la vie intérieure dans *Le Nœud de vipères* de François Mauriac', *Hommage à Pierre Nardin* (Philologie et Littérature Françaises), Annales de la Faculté des Lettres et Sciences Humaines de Nice, no.29, 1977, pp.219–25.
27. Wentersdorf, Karl P., 'The Chronology of Mauriac's *Le Nœud de vipères*', *Kentucky Foreign Language Quarterly*, 13 (1967), supplement, 89–100.

C. OTHER SELECTED WORKS ON MAURIAC

28. *Figures de François Mauriac*, textes par François Trigeaud-Lalanne et photographies par Paul-André Barreau, Bulletin de l'Association des Amis de Marquèze, numéro spécial Année 1985.
29. *François Mauriac: Visions and Reappraisals*, edited by John E. Flower and Bernard C. Swift, Oxford, Berg, 1989.
30. Jenkins, Cecil, *Mauriac*, Edinburgh, Oliver & Boyd, 1965.
31. Lacouture, Jean, *François Mauriac*, Paris, Editions du Seuil, 1980.
32. Mauriac, Claude, *François Mauriac, sa vie, son œuvre*, n.p., Editions Frédéric Birr, 1985.
33. ——, *La Terrasse de Malagar (Le Temps Immobile, 4)*, Paris, Grasset, 1977.
34. Miller, Elinor S., 'The Sacraments in the Novels of François Mauriac', *Renascence*, 31 (1978–79), 168-76.
35. Quoniam, Théodore, *François Mauriac: du péché à la rédemption*, Paris, Téqui, 1984.
36. Simon, Pierre-Henri, *Mauriac par lui-même*, Paris, Editions du Seuil, 1953.
37. Speaight, Robert, *François Mauriac: A Study of the Writer and the Man*, London, Chatto & Windus, 1976.
38. Suffran, Michel, *L'Aquitaine de François Mauriac*, Aix-en-Provence, Edisud, 1983.
39. ——, *François Mauriac ou le regard de la mémoire*, Paris, Colona, 1985.

CRITICAL GUIDES TO FRENCH TEXTS

edited by

Roger Little, Wolfgang van Emden, David Williams